Optical Color Computing: Fuzzy Logic and Digital Calculations

Published 2026 by River Publishers
River Publishers
Broagervej 10, 9260 Gistrup, Denmark
www.riverpublishers.com

Distributed exclusively by Routledge
605 Third Avenue, New York, NY 10017, USA
4 Park Square, Milton Park, Abingdon, Oxon OX14 4RN

Optical Color Computing: Fuzzy Logic and Digital Calculations/by Victor Timchenko, Vladik Kreinovich, Yuriy Kondratenko.

Routledge is an imprint of the Taylor & Francis Group, an informa business

ISBN 978-87-4381-031-5 (paperback)

ISBN 978-87-4381-033-9 (online)

ISBN 978-87-4381-032-2 (ebook master)

ISBN 978-87-4381-035-3 (ePub)

DOI: 10.1201/9788743810322

A Publication in the River Publishers Rapids Series in *Computer Engineering and Information Science and Technology*

Optical Color Computing: Fuzzy Logic and Digital Calculations

Editors

Victor Timchenko

Department of the Computerized Control Systems, Admiral Makarov National University of Shipbuilding, Mykolaiv, Ukraine

Vladik Kreinovich

Department of Computer Science, University of Texas at El Paso, El Paso, TX, USA

Yuriy Kondratenko

Intelligent Information Systems Department, Petro Mohyla Black Sea National University, Mykolaiv Ukraine, and Institute of Artificial Intelligence Problems, Kyiv, Ukraine

River Publishers

Routledge
Taylor & Francis Group
NEW YORK AND LONDON

Contents

Preface

This book (monograph) considers the recent developments of intelligent technologies and methods of optical computing for real-time decision-making systems with a large array of fuzzy input data. The main goals of the developments are:

(a) Increasing the speed of information processing
(b) Expanding the capabilities of parallel computing
(c) Ensuring high reliability of information transmission and processing
(d) Improving the visualization of current output data.

The book consists of two chapters, which were prepared based on a long-term research collaboration between scientists from Ukraine and the United States, in particular, from University of Texas at El Paso, USA, and Admiral Makarov National University of Shipbuilding, Petro Mohyla Black Sea National University, and Institute of Artificial Intelligence Problems, Ukraine.

In the first chapter "Fundamentals of Optical Computing", an in-depth analysis of the main basic principles of optical computing is carried out with the development of a theory of fuzzy data processing, logical operations and conclusions based on the representation of color as an information set and the transformation of light emitters using color filters. Increased efficiency of logical systems is ensured by an innovative approach to the formation and processing of an array of input data based on the use of light radiation of a certain color as a fuzzy variable – a carrier of logical information. This allows for the construction of logical solutions and conclusions by additive and subtractive transformation of light radiation with appropriate light filters, measuring illumination in optical channels and switching light emitters.

The authors of the second chapter "Efficiency and Implementation of Optical Color Computing Architecture in Decision Support Systems" present a comparative analysis of the efficiency of optical color logic devices in processing fuzzy input information in comparison with various algorithms (FPGA, x86-x64, ARM, ARM serial execution) based on the binary representation of fuzzy sets. To implement the proposed optical architecture for constructing a decision support system (DSS), the principles of forming a real-time changing multifactorial fuzzy color database are described. These principles are illustrated on the example of components of a dispatch service for managing intensive traffic of sea ships and/or aircraft. The authors present examples of implementing components of a two-level DSS for traffic safety management and for organizing servicing of sea vessels and aircraft. The results of the performance evaluation of computational operations with fuzzy sets demonstrate a higher speed of optical computations, due to a significantly smaller number of operations and the organization of parallel structures. The authors also provide examples of using logical operations in the DSS to obtain estimates for a certain set of input data. These examples show the effectiveness of the proposed approach.

The results obtained by the authors can be used by large enterprises (mechanical engineering, metalworking, shipbuilding and ship repair, closed-cycle enterprises, raw material extraction, waste recycling, chemical production, etc.) and in infrastructure facilities (airports, seaports, oil and gas terminals, etc.) in various countries where artificial intelligence systems are used for automatic control and decision-making.

The presented results will also be used in theoretical, practical and research training of applicants for higher education in the specialties artificial intelligence, information technology, automation and computer-integrated technologies, electronics and telecommunications, both in Ukrainian and US universities and in educational institutions of other countries.

The chapters of this book have been structured to provide an easy-to-follow introduction to the topics that are addressed, including the most relevant references, so that anyone interested in this field can get started in the area.

We express our deep appreciation to the reviewers for their timely and interesting comments and suggestions.

Editors:

Victor Timchenko, Prof., Dr.Sc., Admiral Makarov National University of Shipbuilding, Ukraine

Vladik Kreinovich, Prof., PhD, Vice President of International Fuzzy Systems Association (IFSA) and Vice President of European Society of Fuzzy Logic and Technology (EUSFLAT)University of Texas at El Paso, USA

Yuriy Kondratenko, Prof., Dr.Sc., Corresponding Academician of the Royal European Academy of Doctors – Barcelona 1914, Corresponding Academician of the RACEF (Spain), Honor Inventor of Ukraine, Petro Mohyla Black Sea National University, and the Institute of Artificial Intelligence Problems, Ukraine

About the Editors

Victor Timchenko received a master's degree in electrical engineering from Admiral Makarov National University of Shipbuilding (AMNUS) in 1982, a philosophy of doctorate degree in design of ships from AMNUS in 1988, and a Doctor of Science degree in automation control from Odessa National Polytechnic University in 2013. He is currently working as a Professor at the Department of Computer Engineering at Automation and Electrical Institute of AMNUS. His research areas include robust optimal control systems, optical architecture and computing, and decision support systems.

Vladik Kreinovich is Professor of Computer Science, University of Texas at El Paso, El Paso, Texas, USA, Vice President of International Fuzzy Systems Association (IFSA) and Vice President of European Society of Fuzzy Logic and Technology (EUSFLAT), and AT&T Fellow in Information Technology. His areas of interest are interval computations, intelligent control (including fuzzy and neural approaches), and reasoning under uncertainty. He is the author of more than 1500 publications.

Yuriy Kondratenko is a Doctor of Science, Professor, Honour Inventor of Ukraine (2008), Corr. Academician of Royal Academy of Doctors (Barcelona, Spain), Head of the Department of Intelligent Information Systems at Petro Mohyla Black Sea National University (PMBSNU), Ukraine, Leading Researcher of the Institute of Artificial Intelligence Problems of MES and NAS of Ukraine, and a Fulbright Scholar. He received a Ph.D. (1983) and Dr.Sc. (1994) from Odessa National Polytechnic University, and several international grants and scholarships for conducting research in P.R. of China, Germany, and the USA. He is Guest Editor of 3 Special Issues of River Publishers Journal of Mobile Multimedia and an Editor of several River Publishers monographs, including Advances in Intelligent Robotics and Collaborative Automation (2015), Control Systems: Theory and Applications (2018), Advanced Control Systems: Theory and Applications (2021), Recent Developments in Automatic Control Systems (2022) and Research Tendencies and Prospect Domains for AI Development and Implementation (2024). Research interests include robotics, automation, sensors and control systems, intelligent decision support systems, and fuzzy logic.

CHAPTER

1

Fundamentals of Optical Computing

V. Timchenko[1] and V. Kreinovich[2]

[1]Department of the Computerized Control Systems, Admiral Makarov National University of Shipbuilding, 9 Heroes of Ukraine Avenue, Mykolaiv 054025, Ukraine
[2]Department of Computer Science, University of Texas at El Paso, 500 W. University, El Paso, TX 78868, USA
E-mail: vl.timchenko58@gmail.com , vladik@utep.edu

Abstract

This chapter considers the forms of representation of a quantum of color information – as a logical component of decision support systems – in the form of operands, matrices and fuzzy sets. An optical computing architecture of logical operations is proposed, which is based on the representation of fuzzy information in the form of quanta of color, the use of optical transformations of ray radiation as natural operations of disjunction and conjunction. It is also the basis for constructing more complex logical operations of decision output. Optical structures of various types of logical "coloroids" implementing various types of decisions and rules of logical inference are formed, and the principles of forming networks of computational coloroids are presented.

Keywords: Information quanta, logic operation, color computing, optical architecture, logical inference.

DOI: 10.1201/9788743810322-1

1.1 Introduction

There are two active trends in the development of computing systems. The first trend is mostly focused on numerical mechanistic, engineering-based calculations based on the desire for maximal accuracy of calculations. The second "humanistic", "qualitative" trend – an example of which is fuzzy calculations [1, 2] – is focused on processing of relevant information and on the construction of decision-making systems with elements of artificial intelligence, systems whose tasks are similar to the tasks performed by human minds.

The first direction, for example in control systems for dynamic objects, suggests the most effective solution in the form of a synthesis of optimal control [3], which involves the following:

- First, it involves the idea of getting maximum knowledge of the structure and parameters of the mathematical model of the control object, as well as of the external disturbances of the working environment. The structure of the model of a dynamic object is usually described by differential equations. These equations are on the laws of mechanics, the only unknown being the parameters, i.e. the coefficients of these differential equations. Because of the need to come up with exact models, the resulting equations provide a simplified description of the actual physical objects. For example, in many situations, these models ignore the effects of air resistance, i.e., in effect, they assume that the objects are moving in a vacuum, or provide a simplified description of the air resistance. In many practical cases, such simplifying assumptions make the resulting models not very accurate. For example, such models are not very accurate when they describe the vessels moving along the sea surface; to accurately describe their motion, we need to take into account the added mass of water (up to 20% of the vessel's mass) that is carried away by the hull of the marine object, and we need to take into account that the hydrodynamic resistance changes during operation due to the fouling of the hull with biomaterial (increasing resistance by 10–15%), etc. In a vacuum, not only is the resistance of the environment absent, but also external disturbances. On the other hand, a marine mobile object is exposed to wind, which is characterized by random gusts, to sea currents, and to irregular (random) sea waves. Knowledge of the model also includes the parameters of external disturbances that can be measured. For a moving marine object, the speeds and directions of wind and currents can be measured quite accurately, while the parameters of sea waves are practically immeasurable. Thus, it can be concluded that the mathematical model of a moving marine object is not fully defined or not fully informative (a softened version of the term "uncertainty"), and is, thus, not absolutely accurate [4]. How accurate should this model be? It depends on the desired accuracy of the control, and this desired accuracy is different in different applications: for example, a spacecraft requires more accurate control than a sea vessel.
- To come up with optimal control, we need to have a clear understanding of which controls are better and we need to have a precise optimality criterion. Coming up with such a criterion is

not easy. For example, for a speedy marine vessel, it makes sense to aim for the maximum speed, and it also make sense to aim for the smallest energy consumption. However, these two requirements are incompatible: the more speed we want to achieve, the more energy we need to spend [5], and in the limit, when the travel time tends to 0 and the speed tends to infinity, the required energy also grows in an unlimited way. Also, the optimality criteria are different in different situations. There are different criteria in normal working conditions, e.g., when a drilling vessel is in the dynamic positioning mode under conditions of a moderately acceptable level of external disturbances, usually up to 5 points, and in extreme situations, when there is a threat of the drilling vessel going beyond the safe zone for technological equipment and critical processes. In this case the survival of the equipment becomes the major objective, and not the speed or energy. In the working mode, the criterion of minimum expended energy is in effect, while in the critical mode we want the minimum time of the transient process.

- We also need to take into account natural constraints. Some of these constraints come from the need to implement this control by using the actual physical engines, and there is a limitation, e.g., on how fast the engine can change its mode.
- It is also important to consider that the physical devices – such as engines – can only implement our instructions with some accuracy, so our control should be sufficiently robust so that it leads to good results even when the actual control values are somewhat different from the ideal planned control schedule.

Because of all these complications, the solution to the optimal control synthesis problem is accurate and optimal only in the ideal world, in which the mathematical model provides the exact description of reality. The actual systems are different from these simplifying models. How can we take into account the difference between the behavior of the actual physical system and of its simplified model? A natural idea is to measure these differences and, based on the empirical data, find the bounds on these differences. Then, instead of looking for the control that is optimal for the exact model, we can use methods of robust-optimal control [3-7] and then look for a control that should perform well for all possible (within-bounds) deviations from the model. For example, we can use minimax techniques – e.g., minimize the worst-case energy consumption, i.e., energy consumption under the worst possible scenario out of all within-bound deviations.

In other words, even when we have uncertainty, we still need to solve a precisely defined optimization problem and, for this purpose, we need to use precise (i.e., very accurate) computations. It is well known that while we humans use decimal numbers, computers use binary numbers that can be grouped together in groups of 3 or 4, thus forming octal or hexadecimal numbers, with bases 8 or 16. From the theoretical viewpoint, the best are ternary numbers, but in terms of practical implementation, binary numbers are the best. This is because, in effect, there is only one technologically simple component with a contactless principle – a transistor – and it has two possible states. For the same reason, it is, as of now, technologically impossible to compete with a transistor in the optical implementation of a binary computing operation, for example, in the form of an optocoupler, despite the obvious advantages in energy costs [8–10]. Engineers have also tried to utilize nonlinear (relay-type) optical effects, for example, effects related to diffraction, interference, polarization. However, in spite of theoretical promise, these efforts are still encountering significant difficulties in implementation [11–20].

Of course, there is also quantum computing, which is based on a completely different physical component – a quantum element. Potentially, quantum computing promises orders of magnitude greater computation speeds. However, in spite of the billions invested in quantum hardware, there are still fundamental difficulties in designing a universal quantum computer. These difficulties are largely due to the uncertain probabilistic nature of quantum effects – most people have heard of Heisenberg's uncertainty principle. As a result, to come up with a reliable computational device, we need to use difficult-to-technologically-implement tricks to compensate for this uncertainty.

Similar difficulties lie in wait for other possible approaches in quantum computing, approaches that try to use the existing quantum objects as elements of the quantum computer instead of trying to manufacture such objects. For example, one possibility is to use the "color" charges of quarks. Many rules for the "color" transformation of quarks–gluons have been formulated and established, so it may be possible, in a distant future, to use quarks for computations. Preliminary ideas on how this can be done are described in our paper [21]. However, this is way beyond our current technology.

Since there are limitations on the first direction, the direction of optimal control, let us analyze the second direction, the direction in which we take into account qualitative information, and in which we design computing based on completely different approaches to the description of information data and functional tasks, and to the process of managing the solution of the set problems. This second approach started with a natural question: is there an absolute need to perform accurate measurements and process numbers when we make decisions? How does a child (or, more broadly, our distant intelligent ancestor), who does not know numbers and letters, perceive input information, and how do they make decisions? Let us cite the reasoning of "an experienced pedestrian" crossing the road [22]. First of all, we estimate the distance to the approaching car, using not numbers, but, for example, the terms "very far", "probably very far", "far", "quite far", "not very close", "nearly", and "very nearly", i.e. we consider only seven terms to be sufficient. Then we estimate the speed of the car, actually recording the time interval and the path traveled by the car during this interval, i.e. differentiating. We will also approximately divide the speed into 7

$\pm$ 2 intervals. And finally, “an experienced pedestrian” realizes his/her errors in determining the accuracy of safety assessments based on the experience of crossing the road, summarizes (integrates) them and stores them in his/her memory, forming an additional signal to increase the speed of crossing the road. “An experienced pedestrian” also represents the degrees of gradation of the sum of his/her errors in the form of a set of intervals.

We have represented “an experienced pedestrian” using linguistic terms [1], which, however, we cannot directly subject to logical transformation, for example, by what rules can we add (perform the disjunction operation) two terms “far” and “quite far” into a natural combination “far or quite far”? Since the words cannot be processed directly, if we want a computer to simulate our reasoning, we are forced to process the words indirectly. Fuzzy technique is how Zadeh proposed to do it. In this technique, we first translate the natural-language terms into “fuzzy sets”, i.e., into what Zadeh called “membership functions”, by assigning, to each value x of the corresponding quantity (e.g., distance), a degree to which we believe that this value satisfies the given property, i.e., to which this object at a distance x is far, Then, we process these membership functions by using transformations corresponding to “and”, “or”, etc., and at the end, if we want to formulate an advice for a human being, we translate the resulting processed membership function back into natural.

This is a very time-consuming computational process. Can we do it faster? By the way, it is worth noting that the introduction of linguistic terms is also not necessary: it is obvious that a person who does not know the alphabet also reacts to danger with some organ of the human mind and visual sensor and distributes its degrees.

Let us determine how the simplest logical inference is organized based on the above-mentioned “experienced pedestrian”. The goal is defined – to cross the road. Having collected (summed up, which is a logical operation of disjunction $\vee$) the main factors for this, for example, the absence of a traffic light at a pedestrian crossing, good weather and time of day, the pedestrian makes a decision to cross, but passes this decision (subtraction, which is a logical operation of conjunction $\wedge$) through a kind of filter of estimates of the distance to the car, its speed and accumulated error (Figure 1.1). And then he/she makes the final decision.

In fact, the resulting inference system needs only the two logical operations of disjunction and conjunction. The logical operation of “negation” is essentially the adoption of a new decision, a forced “voluntaristic” operation, in contrast to a logical decision resulting from given estimates. So, it can be assumed that the first two logical operations will be widely and often applicable

Figure 1.1: Logical scheme of the "experienced pedestrian" decision.

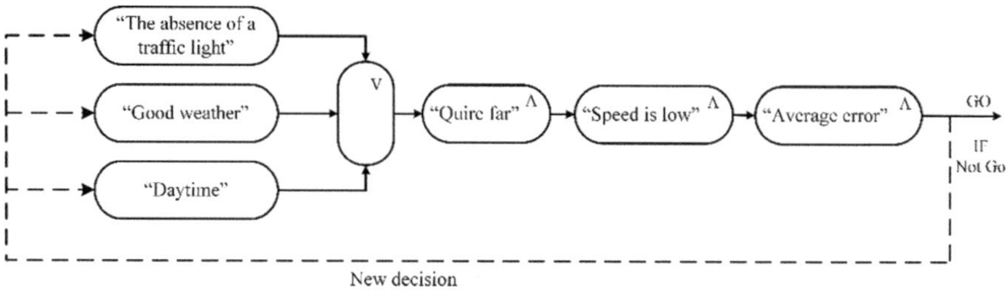

in decision making, and the operation of negation will be quite rare. Such an inference can be used as a basis for creating architectural components for "qualitative", fuzzy calculations, easily implemented (and note, without switching) for the first two logical operations, but at the same time allowing for some implementation complexities and logical switching.

1.2 Color is a Quantum of Information

In the previous section, we argued that the current methods of processing information are too complicated and therefore too slow. How can we process information faster than modern computers can? One way to be faster is to use the fastest possible processes for computing, and, according to special relativity, the fastest possible process is light (and, more generally, electromagnetic waves). So, a natural idea is to use light for computing.

To use light, we need to be able to describe light in precise terms. To describe a ray of light, we need to know two things: its intensity and its color. Intensity is just a number, but how can we describe light? To answer this question, let us go back in time.

The concept of color has attracted and accompanied man, apparently, since the moment he saw a rainbow. It is not surprising that, for example, in the Ukrainian language, one of the words for the rainbow – raiduha – literally means "the arc of paradise". For a long time, humanity was burdened with more significant concerns such as the formation of civilization, the struggle for food, the development of religions, languages, and technologies. Color, of course, played a role in clothing and art, instinctively expressing emotions of perception of aggression, challenge (red, yellow), and peace (blue, green), but this was rather superficial and intuitive in nature. The main attention in the development of optics in this period was paid to geometric optics and the improvement of lenses and mirrors. Only after the technological industrial revolution of the 18th and 19th centuries did another revolution, already pictorial and cultural, appear in the works of a galaxy of impressionist artists. Here, already, clearly, color had acquired an informational load. It contained information, on the canvas, about the movement of people and the environment, the emotions of the characters, the dynamics of the plot, etc. Artists, again rather intuitively, but at the same time brilliantly, recognized and showed that the surrounding world contains previously hidden information – information described by colors.

At that time, practically in parallel (from the historical viewpoint) with the work of the impressionists, the science of optical phenomena was developing, first by I. Newton, R. Hooke, H. Huygens and others, then by T. Young, O. Fresnel, F. Arago and others. The relation between physical colors and human perception of the visible spectrum of light was studied by researchers called coloristics: G. Grassmann, R. Runge and others [23–28]. Thanks to their work, the optical phenomena of diffraction, interference, and polarization of light radiation were explained. Then, by the work of D. Maxwell, M. Planck, A. Einstein (and other, no less famous scientists), a more general phenomenon of electromagnetic and photonic duality of the nature of light was discovered, which led to the creation of the general theory of quantum optics. Let us note a very important outgrowth of quantum optics, which received the name of quantum chromodynamics. This theory assumes that elementary particles of quarks have a certain "color" charge, subject, in effect, to the laws of coloristics of the visible spectrum of light radiation.

So why not use light – in particular, colored light – to process information? With the emergence of computers that processed numbers but – at that time – rather slowly, researchers tried to use optical systems to perform the same computations faster. Such systems were developed for, in particular fuzzy-related computational tasks. The problem was that these devices required so many components – lenses, prisms, complex diffraction gratings, additional devices in the form of piezoelectric crystal elements and optoelectronic phase shifters, coding systems, holograms, shadow images, etc. – that for reasonably complex problems, problems for which there was a real need to speed up, optical computation became impractical.

Since we cannot directly use light – in particular colored light – to perform, step by step, whatever computational steps we use in a computer, a natural idea is to use it differently. We humans do not use numbers in our everyday decision making, we use discrete quanta of information – that the distance is far, that the speed is slow. So why not use colored light to describe these information quanta.

When we ourselves think about colors – and make conclusions about colors – we do not use numbers. This says something – after all, we humans are a result of billions of years of improving evolution, so whatever happens in our bodies and in our brains has been probably tested and re-tested by nature and found to be good. So maybe a good idea is to start our ideas of optical computing by emulating how we perceive and process colors, and, while we are doing it, let us relate our thoughts, if possible, to how computers do it. We started thinking about all in an earlier paper [22], but now we have a more general understanding of how this can be done. So let us describe this more general understanding.

It is known that we perceive each color as a combination of three basic colors – red, green, and blue. This is how computers represent color. We can have black, meaning that there is no color at all, we can have white, which is a combination of all three colors, and we can also have combinations of two colors, which lead to magenta, cyan, and yellow – a total of eight colors; see Table 1.1. Each of these colors can be described by specifying, for each of the three basic colors – red, green, and blue – whether this basic color is present (1) or absent (0). Thus, each color is represented by a 3-digit binary number. These numbers go from 000 which is 0, to 111 which is 7 – the eight numbers forming the octal (8-based) number system.

Table 1.1: Converting alphabet to numbers.

Color		Set	Number
Black		[0, 0, 0]	0
Red		[0, 0, 1]	1
Green		[0, 1, 0]	2
Yellow		[0, 1, 1]	3
Blue		[1, 0, 0]	4
Magenta		[1, 0, 1]	5
Cyan		[1, 1, 0]	6
White		[1, 1, 1]	7

This way, we can represent each octal number, i.e., a sequence of octal digits 0 through 7, as a sequence of colors.

Now we represent colors by numbers, and the numerical value of a color is obtained by adding the numerical values of its component basic colors.

$$R + G = Yel \to 1 + 2 = 3;$$
$$R + B = M \to 1 + 4 = 5;$$
$$G + Yel = M \to 2 + 3 = 5;$$
$$R + G = Yel \to 1 + 2 = 3;$$
$$B + G = C \to 4 + 2 = 6;$$
$$M + G = W \to 5 + 2 = 7;$$
$$R + C = W \to 1 + 6 = 7;$$
$$R + G + B = W \to 1 + 2 + 4 = 7;$$
$$W - R - G - B = Blc \to 7 - 1 - 2 - 4 = 0.$$

What happens when we try to combine two general colors – not necessarily basic ones? In this case, we can still use the same plus symbol + for this combination, but this will no longer be the usual addition. For example, if we add two rays of the same color, we still get the same color: $1 + 1 = 1, 2 + 2 = 2$; this is known as idempotence. Here are other examples when a combination of two colors differs from the usual addition:

$$R + Yel = Yel \to 1 + 3 \neq 3;$$
$$R + R = R \to 1 + 1 \neq 1.$$

This means, by the way, that it is not possible to base simple optical color transformations on arithmetic computational operations, and it is necessary to seek other physical principles for these purposes.

Instead of combining basic colors, we can consider possible states of a triple of objects each of which can be in one of the basic colors. This leads to $3^3 = 27$ possibilities (see Table 1.2), which, is, interestingly, close to 26, the number of letters in the standard Latin alphabet. We can similarly use 27 possible combinations of three mixed colors – magenta, cyan, and yellow – to describe syntactic signs like point, comma, etc.

This way, any text, i.e., a sequence of symbols, can be represented as a sequence of colors.

We believe that color representation of text information, in addition to encoding and transmitting information, also has possible positive psychological aspects, revealing and expanding the creative potential of the human mind; this idea, of course, requires additional research.

Table 1.2: Converting alphabet and syntax sign to colors.

Serial number	Letter	Color set			Syntax sign	Color set		
1	A	R	R	G	.	Y	Y	M
2	B	B	B	B	,	C	C	C
3	C	B	B	G	!	C	C	M
4	D	G	R	R	?	M	Y	Y
5	E	R	R	B	;	Y	Y	C
6	F	B	R	R	:	C	Y	Y
7	G	R	B	B	“	Y	C	C
8	H	B	R	B	‘	C	Y	C
9	I	B	B	R	)	C	C	Y
10	J	G	G	R	(	M	M	Y
11	K	G	R	G	+	M	Y	M
12	L	B	R	G	_	C	Y	M
13	M	R	B	G	-	Y	C	M
14	N	G	R	B	=	M	Y	C
15	O	R	G	B	%	Y	M	C
16	P	G	G	G	#	M	M	M
17	Q	G	B	R	@	M	C	Y
18	R	B	G	R	<	C	M	Y
19	S	R	R	R	>	Y	Y	Y
20	T	R	G	G	&	Y	M	M
21	U	R	B	B	\	Y	C	C
22	V	G	B	G	/	M	C	M
23	W	B	G	B	–	C	M	C
24	X	G	G	B	*	M	M	C
25	Y	B	G	G	∨	C	M	M
26	Z	G	B	B	∧	M	C	C
27					→	Y	M	Y

Let's consider the applicability of color optical transformation to the implementation of basic logical operations – disjunction, conjunction, negation, and their combinations.

Let's form a sufficiently complete representation of the necessary input data, for example, in relation to a positive assessment (conclusion), as a basis for building decision support systems: complete negation of a positive assessment; very possible negation; rather negative assessment; rather positive assessment; very possibly positive assessment; completely positive assessment (Figure 1.2). Obviously, this is qualitative, fuzzy information.

Figure 1.2: Linguistic terms (gradation of assessments) for representation of the necessary input data.

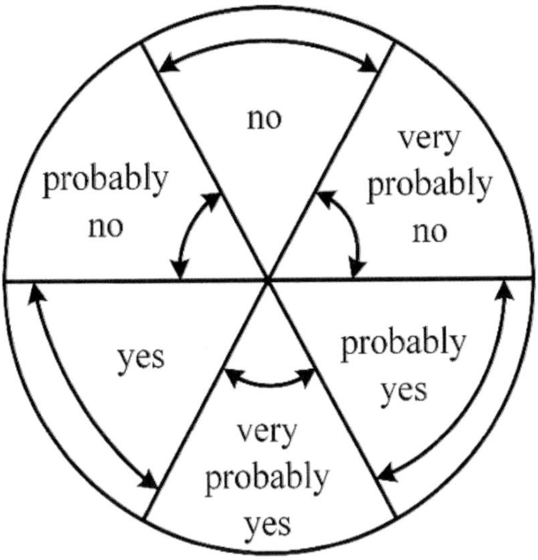

It is also logical to put the proposed gradation of assessments in the form of six values, respectively, three primary and three additional colors, depicted on the circular diagram of Figure 1.3.

How can these degrees of confidence be related to colors? We are accustomed to red meaning "no". It seems reasonable to describe "yes" as a color on the other side of the spectrum, i.e., blue.

In the spectrum, green is closer to blue than to red, so we can say that it is somewhat positive – what we described as "probably yes".

What about mixed colors? Cyan is a combination of green and blue, so the degree corresponding to cyan should be in between the degrees corresponding to blue and green, i.e., between "yes" and "possibly yes". Out of our seven possible degrees, there is only one degree between "yes" and "possibly yes": the degree "very possibly yes". So, this will be the degree corresponding to cyan.

Figure 1.3: Circular diagram with gradation of assessments representation by colors.

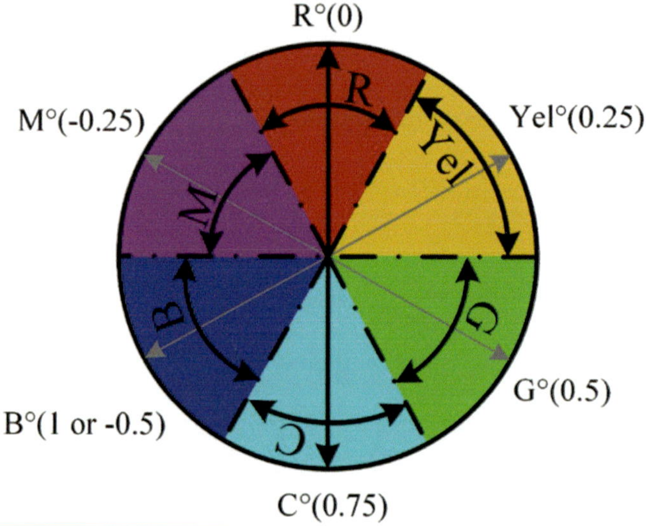

What degree should correspond to magenta? Magenta is a combination of red ("yes") and blue ("no"). This seems to indicate something neutral, something that is strictly in between "yes" and "no", but we do not have such a degree, so this must be something close to neutral – either "possibly yes" or "possibly no". We already have a color equivalent to a "possibly yes" – which is cyan. So, the only choice for magenta is "possibly no".

Now, we have one un-matched color, yellow, and the only unmatched degree, "very possibly no". So, it is natural to match them with each other. This matching is in perfect accordance with all the others: indeed, green is in between red and blue, so yellow (red + green) should be in between red (red + red) which is "no" and magenta (red + blue) which is "possibly no". Thus, the degree corresponding to yellow should be between "no" and "possibly no", and there is only one such degree, which is exactly "very possibly no".

Now, the only un-matched are the two no-color combinations: black and white. To match them, we have two options: (positive) decision and no decision. Intuitively, decision sounds more positive than no decision, and white sounds more positive than black, so it is natural to associate white with positive decision and black with no decision. Thus, we arrive at Table 1.3.

Table 1.3: Degrees of confidence.

Color	Degrees of confidence
$\{R\}$	"no"
$\{G\}$	"probably yes"
$\{B\}$	"yes"
$\{W\} = \{R\} + \{G\} + \{B\}$	"positive decision"
$\{C\} = \{G\} + \{B\} = \{G, B\}$	"very probably yes"
$\{M\} = \{R\} + \{B\} = \{R, B\}$	"probably no"
$\{Yel\} = \{R\} + \{G\} = \{R, G\}$	"very probably no"
$\{Blc\} = \{W\} - \{R\} - \{G\} - \{B\}$	"no decision"

1.3 Mathematical Representation of Color Information Sets

We can use the disjunction and conjunction operations directly [29–35], representing the information sets with the appropriate color (Table 1.3).

By introducing the logical operands of falsehood **N** for **R** and truth **Y** for **B**, and for **G**, respectively, **YN**, we can form color sets using the basic operations of summation and subtraction of color radiations using the appropriate color filters, for example,

$$\begin{aligned}
\{C\} &= \{G\}+\{B\}\rightarrow\{YN\}+\{Y\}=\{YYN\};\\
\{M\} &= \{R\}+\{B\}\rightarrow\{N\}+\{Y\}=\{NY\};\\
\{Yel\} &= \{R\}+\{G\}\rightarrow\{N\}+\{YN\}=\{NYN\};\\
\{W\} &= \{R\}+\{G\}+\{B\}\rightarrow\{N\}+\{YN\}+\{Y\}=\{NYNY\};\\
\{Blc\} &= \{W\}-\{R\}-\{G\}-\{B\}\rightarrow\{NYNY\}-\{N\}-\{YN\}-\{Y\}=\{0\}.
\end{aligned} \tag{1}$$

In this case, some features of the use of operands should be taken into account: green radiation, although it contains **N** in the operands, will not pass, unlike magenta radiation, through the red filter (an optical property of primary color filters). When using subtraction (conjunction), the subtracted color is blocked by the filter for primary colors. For example, when blue passes through a red filter $\{R\}$, blue $\{B\}$ is blocked and there is no light radiation at the filter output $\{Blc\} = \{0\}$, so it is correct to write this operation as follows:

$$\{R\} \wedge \{B\} = \{N\} - \{N\} = \{0\}.$$

We can also use a matrix representation of the color set [32]

$$\begin{aligned}
&\{R\} \rightarrow diag\,(R, 0,\ 0);\ \{G\} \rightarrow diag\,(0, G,\ 0);\ \{B\} \rightarrow diag\,(0,\ 0,\ B);\\
&\{Yel\} \rightarrow diag\,(R, G,\ 0);\ \{C\} \rightarrow diag\,(0, G,\ B);\ \{M\} \rightarrow diag\,(R,\ 0,\ B);\\
&\{W\} \rightarrow diag\,(R, G,\ B);\ \{Blc\} \rightarrow diag\,(0, 0,\ 0).
\end{aligned} \tag{2}$$

Expanding the functionality of logical operations with algebraic summation and product, the paper [33] shows a representation of color sets in the form of membership functions. For example, red means "no", so the membership degree of "red" for the "no" in fuzzy logic, i.e., for the value 0, is 1. Also, all the values smaller than 0.25, which is our next level, should also correspond to "no", so we assign 1 as a membership degree for some value 0.25 minus some small number σ. Similarly, green, which is in between "yes" and "no", should have degree 1 for the intermediate value 0.5 and for the values close to the endpoints of the corresponding interval around 0.5, i.e., to the points $0.75 - \sigma$ and $0.25 + \sigma$. As a result, we get the following membership functions:

$$\begin{aligned}
\{R\} &= \frac{1}{-0.25+\sigma} + \frac{1}{0} + \frac{1}{0.25-\sigma};\\
\{G\} &= \frac{1}{0.25+\sigma} + \frac{1}{0.5} + \frac{1}{0.75-\sigma};\\
\{B\} &= \frac{1}{0.75+\sigma} + \frac{1}{1} + \frac{1}{-0.25-\sigma};\\
\{Yel\} &= \frac{0.5}{-0.25+\sigma} + \frac{1}{0} + \frac{0.5}{0.25-\sigma} + \frac{0.5}{0.25+\sigma} + \frac{1}{0.5} + \frac{0.5}{0.75-\sigma};\\
\{C\} &= \frac{0.5}{0.25+\sigma} + \frac{1}{0.5} + \frac{0.5}{0.75-\sigma} + \frac{0.5}{0.75+\sigma} + \frac{1}{1} + \frac{0.5}{-0.25-\sigma};\\
\{M\} &= \frac{0.5}{-0.25+\sigma} + \frac{1}{0} + \frac{0.5}{0.25\ \ \sigma} + \frac{0.5}{0.75+\sigma} + \frac{1}{1} + \frac{0.5}{-0.25-\sigma};\\
\{W\} &= \frac{1}{0} + \frac{1}{0.25} + \frac{1}{0.5} + \frac{1}{0.75} + \frac{1}{1} + \frac{1}{-0.25};\\
\{Blc\} &= \neg\{W\} = \frac{0}{-0.25} + \frac{0}{0} + \frac{0}{0.25} + \frac{0}{0.5} + \frac{0}{0.75} + \frac{0}{1},
\end{aligned} \tag{3}$$

where σ is a small parameter [33].

1.4 Basic Color Logical Operations

Let us consider the properties of the basic logical operations – associativity, commutativity, absorptivity, distributivity, additionality, idempotence – based on additive and subtractive optical color transformation (1–3), respectively using the operations of disjunction and conjunction (*a*), operands $\{Y\}$ and $\{N\}$ (*b*), diagonal matrices (*c*), and fuzzy sets (*d*).

1.4.1 Commutativity

The sum of the $\{R\}$ and $\{B\}$ color produces magenta for both combinations, just as a red filter blocks blue, and a blue filter blocks red:

(a)

$$\{R\} \vee \{B\} = \{B\} \vee \{R\}, \{R\} \wedge \{B\} = \{B\} \wedge \{R\};$$

(b)

$$\{N\} + \{Y\} = \{Y\} + \{N\}, \{N\} - \{Y\} = \{Y\} - \{N\};$$

(c)

$$diag\,(R,\ 0,\ 0) + diag\,(0,\ 0,\ B) = diag\,(0,\ 0,\ B) + diag\,(R,\ 0,\ 0)\,;$$
$$diag\,(R,\ 0,\ 0) \times diag\,(0,\ 0,\ B) = diag\,(0,\ 0,\ B) \times diag\,(R,\ 0,\ 0)\,;$$

(d)

$$\left(\frac{1}{-0.25+\sigma}+\frac{1}{0}+\frac{1}{0.25-\sigma}\right) \vee \left(\frac{1}{0.75+\sigma}+\frac{1}{1}+\frac{1}{-0.25-\sigma}\right)$$
$$= \left(\frac{1}{0.75+\sigma}+\frac{1}{1}+\frac{1}{-0.25-\sigma}\right) \vee \left(\frac{1}{-0.25+\sigma}+\frac{1}{0}+\frac{1}{0.25-\sigma}\right);$$
$$\left(\frac{1}{-0.25+\sigma}+\frac{1}{0}+\frac{1}{0.25-\sigma}\right) \wedge \left(\frac{1}{0.75+\sigma}+\frac{1}{1}+\frac{1}{-0.25-\sigma}\right)$$
$$= \left(\frac{1}{0.75+\sigma}+\frac{1}{1}+\frac{1}{-0.25-\sigma}\right) \wedge \left(\frac{1}{-0.25+\sigma}+\frac{1}{0}+\frac{1}{0.25-\sigma}\right).$$

1.4.2 Associativity

In any combination, the sum of the colors will give white, and subtraction will give black.

(a)

$$\{R\} \vee (\{B\} \vee \{G\}) = (\{R\} \vee \{B\}) \vee \{G\};$$
$$\{R\} \wedge (\{B\} \wedge \{G\}) = (\{R\} \wedge \{B\}) \wedge \{G\};$$

(b)

$$\{N\} + (\{Y\} + \{YN\}) = (\{N\} + \{Y\}) + \{YN\}\,;$$
$$\{N\} - (\{Y\} - \{YN\}) = (\{N\} - \{Y\}) - \{YN\};$$

(c)

$$diag\,(R,\ 0,\ 0) + [diag\,(0,\ 0,\ B) + diag\,(0,\ G,\ 0)] =$$
$$= [diag\,(0,\ 0,\ B) + diag\,(R,\ 0,\ 0)] + diag\,(0,\ G,\ 0)\,;$$
$$diag\,(R,\ 0,\ 0) \times [diag\,(0,\ 0,\ B) \times diag\,(0,\ G,\ 0)] =$$
$$= [diag\,(0,\ 0,\ B) \times diag\,(R,\ 0,\ 0)] \times diag\,(0,\ G,\ 0)\,;$$

(d)

$$\left(\frac{1}{-0.25+\sigma}+\frac{1}{0}+\frac{1}{0.25-\sigma}\right)\vee\left[\left(\frac{1}{0.75+\sigma}+\frac{1}{1}+\frac{1}{-0.25-\sigma}\right)\right.$$
$$\left.\vee\left(\frac{1}{0.25+\sigma}+\frac{1}{0.5}+\frac{1}{0.75-\sigma}\right)\right]$$
$$=\left[\left(\frac{1}{-0.25+\sigma}+\frac{1}{0}+\frac{1}{0.25-\sigma}\right)\vee\left(\frac{1}{0.75+\sigma}+\frac{1}{1}+\frac{1}{-0.25-\sigma}\right)\right]$$
$$\vee\left(\frac{1}{0.25+\sigma}+\frac{1}{0.5}+\frac{1}{0.75-\sigma}\right)\ ;$$
$$\left(\frac{1}{-0.25+\sigma}+\frac{1}{0}+\frac{1}{0.25-\sigma}\right)\wedge\left[\left(\frac{1}{0.75+\sigma}+\frac{1}{1}+\frac{1}{-0.25-\sigma}\right)\right.$$
$$\left.\wedge\left(\frac{1}{0.25+\sigma}+\frac{1}{0.5}+\frac{1}{0.75-\sigma}\right)\right]$$
$$=\left(\frac{1}{-0.25+\sigma}+\frac{1}{0}+\frac{1}{0.25-\sigma}\right)\wedge\left(\frac{1}{0.75+\sigma}+\frac{1}{1}+\frac{1}{-0.25-\sigma}\right)$$
$$\wedge\left(\frac{1}{0.25+\sigma}+\frac{1}{0.5}+\frac{1}{0.75-\sigma}\right).$$

1.4.3 Absorptivity

For the first formula, taking a magenta color and passing it through a blue filter produces blue, for the second formula, red light passing through blue is blocked, and no color and blue produces blue color.

(a)

$$(\{R\}\vee\{B\})\wedge\{B\}=\{B\}\,,(\{R\}\wedge\{B\})\vee\{B\}=\{B\};$$

(b)

$$(\{N\}+\{Y\})-\{N\}=\{Y\}\,,\{N\}-\{N\}+\{Y\}=\{Y\};$$

(c)

$$[diag\,(R,\ 0,\ 0)+diag\,(0,\ 0,\ B)]\times diag\,(0,\ 0,\ B)=diag\,(0,\ 0,\ B)\,;$$
$$[diag\,(R,\ 0,\ 0)\times diag\,(0,\ 0,\ B)]+diag\,(0,\ 0,\ B)=diag\,(0,\ 0,\ B)\,;$$

(d)

$$\left[\left(\frac{1}{-0.25+\sigma}+\frac{1}{0}+\frac{1}{0.25-\sigma}\right)\vee\left(\frac{1}{0.75+\sigma}+\frac{1}{1}+\frac{1}{-0.25-\sigma}\right)\right]$$
$$\wedge\left(\frac{1}{0.75+\sigma}+\frac{1}{1}+\frac{1}{-0.25-\sigma}\right)=\{B\};$$
$$\left(\frac{1}{-0.25+\sigma}+\frac{1}{0}+\frac{1}{0.25-\sigma}\right)\wedge\left(\frac{1}{0.75+\sigma}+\frac{1}{1}+\frac{1}{-0.25-\sigma}\right)$$
$$\vee\left(\frac{1}{0.75+\sigma}+\frac{1}{1}+\frac{1}{-0.25-\sigma}\right)=\{B\}.$$

1.4.4 Distributivity

In the first case we get a red color for this combination, in the second, the absence of light.

(a)

$$\{R\}\vee(\{B\}\wedge\{G\})=(\{R\}\vee\{B\})\wedge(\{R\}\vee\{G\});$$
$$\{R\}\wedge(\{B\}\vee\{G\})=(\{R\}\wedge\{B\})\vee(\{R\}\wedge\{G\}); \tag{4}$$

(b)

$$\{N\}+(\{Y\}-\{YN\})=(\{N\}+\{Y\})-(\{N\}+\{YN\})=\{N\};$$
$$\{N\}-(\{Y\}+\{YN\})=(\{N\}-\{Y\})+(\{N\}-\{YN\})=\{0\};$$

(c)

$$diag\,(R,\ 0,\ 0)+[diag\,(0,\ 0,\ B)\times diag\,(0,\ G,\ 0)]=[diag\,(R,\ 0,\ 0)$$
$$+diag\,(0,\ 0,\ B)]\times[diag\,(R,\ 0,\ 0)+diag\,(0,\ G,\ 0)]=diag\,(R,\ 0,\ 0);$$
$$diag\,(R,\ 0,\ 0)\times[diag\,(0,\ 0,\ B)+diag\,(0,\ G,\ 0)]=[diag\,(R,\ 0,\ 0)$$
$$\times diag\,(0,\ 0,\ B)].+[diag\,(R,\ 0,\ 0)\times diag\,(0,\ G,\ 0)]=diag\,(0,\ 0,\ 0);$$

(d)

$$\left(\frac{1}{-0.25+\sigma}+\frac{1}{0}+\frac{1}{0.25-\sigma}\right)\vee\left[\left(\frac{1}{0.75+\sigma}+\frac{1}{1}+\frac{1}{-0.25-\sigma}\right)\right.$$
$$\left.\wedge\left(\frac{1}{0.25+\sigma}+\frac{1}{0.5}+\frac{1}{0.75-\sigma}\right)\right]=\left[\left(\frac{1}{-0.25+\sigma}+\frac{1}{0}+\frac{1}{0.25-\sigma}\right)\right.$$
$$\left.\wedge\left(\frac{1}{0.75+\sigma}+\frac{1}{1}+\frac{1}{-0.25-\sigma}\right)\right]\vee\left[\left(\frac{1}{-0.25+\sigma}+\frac{1}{0}+\frac{1}{0.25-\sigma}\right)\right.$$

$$\wedge\left(\frac{1}{0.25+\sigma}+\frac{1}{0.5}+\frac{1}{0.75-\sigma}\right)\Bigg]=\{R\};\left(\frac{1}{-0.25+\sigma}+\frac{1}{0}+\frac{1}{0.25-\sigma}\right)$$
$$\wedge\left[\left(\frac{1}{0.75+\sigma}+\frac{1}{1}+\frac{1}{-0.25-\sigma}\right)\vee\left(\frac{1}{0.25+\sigma}+\frac{1}{0.5}+\frac{1}{0.75-\sigma}\right)\right]$$
$$=\left[\left(\frac{1}{-0.25+\sigma}+\frac{1}{0}+\frac{1}{0.25-\sigma}\right)\vee\left(\frac{1}{0.75+\sigma}+\frac{1}{1}+\frac{1}{-0.25-\sigma}\right)\right]$$
$$\wedge\left[\left(\frac{1}{-0.25+\sigma}+\frac{1}{0}+\frac{1}{0.25-\sigma}\right)\vee\left(\frac{1}{0.25+\sigma}+\frac{1}{0.5}+\frac{1}{0.75-\sigma}\right)\right]=\{0\}.$$

1.4.5 Additionality

If we define a light emitter as opposite (i.e. *Blc*} = ¬{*W*}), then the additionality property will be satisfied:

(a)

$$(\{Blc\}\vee\neg\{Blc\})\wedge\{W\}=\{W\},(\{Blc\}\wedge\neg\{Blc\})\vee\{W\}=\{W\};$$

(b)

$$(\{0\}+\neg\{0\})-\{YYNN\}=\{YYNN\},(\{0\}-\neg\{0\})+\{YYNN\}$$
$$=\{YYNN\};$$

(c)

$$[diag\,(0,\ 0,\ 0)+diag\,(R,G,\ B)]\times diag\,(R,G,\ B)=diag\,(R,G,\ B)\,;$$
$$[diag\,(0,\ 0,\ 0)\times diag\,(R,G,\ B)]+diag\,(R,G,\ B)=diag\,(R,G,\ B)\,;$$

(d)

$$\left[\left(\frac{0}{-0.25}+\frac{0}{0}+\frac{0}{0.25}+\frac{0}{0.5}+\frac{0}{0.75}+\frac{0}{1}\right)\right.$$
$$\left.\vee\left(\frac{1}{0}+\frac{1}{0.25}+\frac{1}{0.5}+\frac{1}{0.75}+\frac{1}{1}+\frac{1}{-0.25}\right)\right]$$
$$\wedge\left(\frac{1}{0}+\frac{1}{0.25}+\frac{1}{0.5}+\frac{1}{0.75}+\frac{1}{1}+\frac{1}{-0.25}\right)=\{W\};$$
$$\left[\left(\frac{0}{-0.25}+\frac{0}{0}+\frac{0}{0.25}+\frac{0}{0.5}+\frac{0}{0.75}+\frac{0}{1}\right)\right.$$
$$\left.\wedge\left(\frac{1}{0}+\frac{1}{0.25}+\frac{1}{0.5}+\frac{1}{0.75}+\frac{1}{1}+\frac{1}{-0.25}\right)\right]$$
$$\vee\left(\frac{1}{0}+\frac{1}{0.25}+\frac{1}{0.5}+\frac{1}{0.75}+\frac{1}{1}+\frac{1}{-0.25}\right)=\{W\}.$$

1.4.6 Idempotence

Summing the color does not change the color, nor does passing the color through a filter of the same color.

(a)

$$\{R\} \vee \{R\} = \{R\}, \{R\} \wedge \{R\} = \{R\};$$

(b)

$$\{N\} + \{N\} = \{N\}, \{N\} - \{N\} = \{N\};$$

(c)

$$diag\,(R,\ 0,\ 0) + diag\,(R,\ 0,\ 0) = diag\,(R,\ 0,\ 0)\,;$$

$$diag\,(R,\ 0,\ 0) \times diag\,(R,\ 0,\ 0) = diag\,(R,\ 0,\ 0)\,;$$

(d)

$$\left(\frac{1}{-0.25+\sigma}+\frac{1}{0}+\frac{1}{0.25-\sigma}\right) \vee \left(\frac{1}{-0.25+\sigma}+\frac{1}{0}+\frac{1}{0.25-\sigma}\right) = \{R\};$$

$$\left(\frac{1}{-0.25+\sigma}+\frac{1}{0}+\frac{1}{0.25-\sigma}\right) \wedge \left(\frac{1}{-0.25+\sigma}+\frac{1}{0}+\frac{1}{0.25-\sigma}\right) = \{R\}.$$

1.5 Optical Color Computing Architecture

1.5.1 Elementary and basic logical coloroids

The simplest elementary logical operations are formed by additive and subtractive optical transformations of light radiation. Additive transformation of light radiation of certain colors determines the disjunction operation for the corresponding information sets. Optically, the additive summation block is realized by an adder of the required number of light guides with light radiation of a given color (Figure 1.4).

The logical operation of disjunction has for the input signal $\{W\}$ seven non-repeating variants of output information quanta;$\{W\}$, $\{R\}$, $\{G\}$, $\{B\}$, $\{Yel\}$, $\{M\}$, $\{C\}$, and in matrix form looks like this:

$$diag\,(R, 0, 0) + diag\,(0, G, 0) + diag\,(0, 0, B) = diag\,(R, G, B)\,.$$

The subtractive transformation defines the conjunction operation and is optically implemented by a subtraction unit (Figure 1.5) based on light guides

Figure 1.4: Additive summation block.

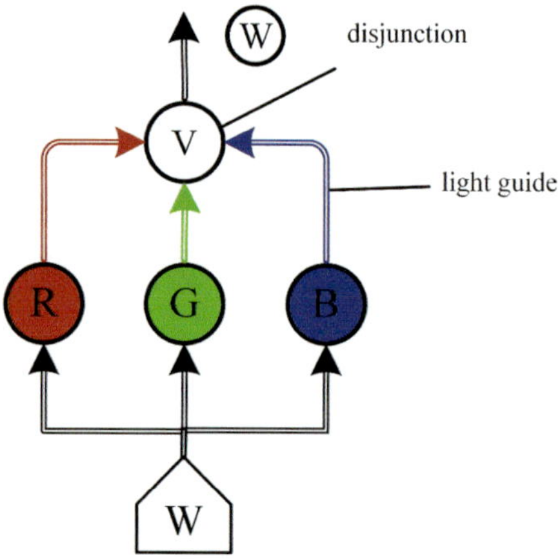

Figure 1.5: Subtraction unit.

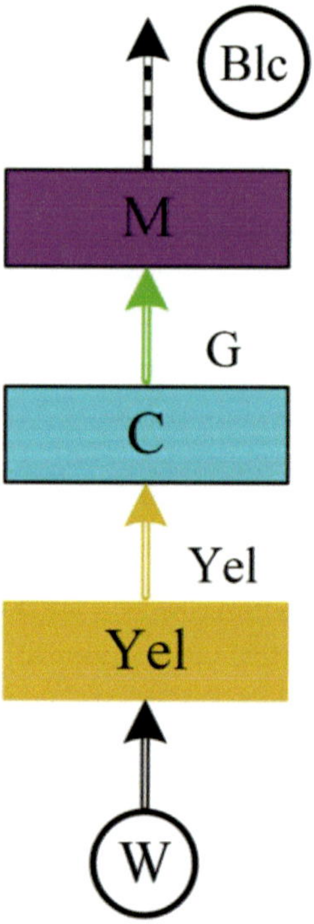

with transversely located filters of a certain color, specified by the corresponding expert or sensory assessments or measurements, and filtering the light radiation in accordance with the specified logical operations.

The logical conjunction operation for this optical scheme has 49 non-repeating combinations for seven variants of input information quanta and is written in matrix form for the combination of color filters **Yel**, **M**, **C** and the input quantum$\{W\}$

$$diag\,(R,\ G,\ B) \times diag\,(R,\ G,\ 0) \times diag\,(0,\ G,\ B) \times diag\,(R,\ 0,\ B)$$
$$= diag\,(0,0,0)\,.$$

At the output of the subtractive coloroid we will also have seven variants of information light quanta:$\{Blc\}$, $\{R\}$, $\{G\}$, $\{B\}$, $\{Yel\}$, $\{M\}$, $\{C\}$.

Introducing the logic of decision-making, for example, based on expert assessments, we assumed an acceptable minimum number of experts and their hierarchy. The first level of such a basic optical-logical device (we use the name "coloroid", combining logic and color) includes assessments of three "main" experts. It is the "main" experts who form the necessary variants of the summed assessments – "yes", "no", rather "yes".

The predominance of positive assessments is explained by the fact that the decision-making process is initially configured to make a positive action (decision) on a certain task, but naturally, with negative assessments, the decision will be negative. Next, we introduce six additional "coordinating experts", placing them 2 by 2 in three parallel branches converging in optical summation. Coordinating experts refine the assessment (decision) of the primary main experts, optically filtering the information specified by a certain color. Parallel branches and light filters of additional colors reduce the possibility of blocking the assessment (decision) in this (second) optical section. Research aimed at optimizing the colorimetric structure has shown [32] that the use of three branches takes into account both the need for alternative solutions and the minimum median spread of their estimates. The third optical section includes three light filters connected serially by light guides; this forms the final decision (assessment) at the output by three "responsible" experts, for example, those bearing personal liability of one kind or another. If an expert is personally responsible, e.g., for safety, then the conclusion of this expert that the decision may lead to an unsafe situation will automatically block this decision. On the other hand, if a different expert, who is not legally liable for any specific aspect of the decision, they simply expressed their somewhat negative opinion, it is still possible that the overall positive decision will be made, e.g., if all other experts

Figure 1.6: Optical structure of the base coloroid.

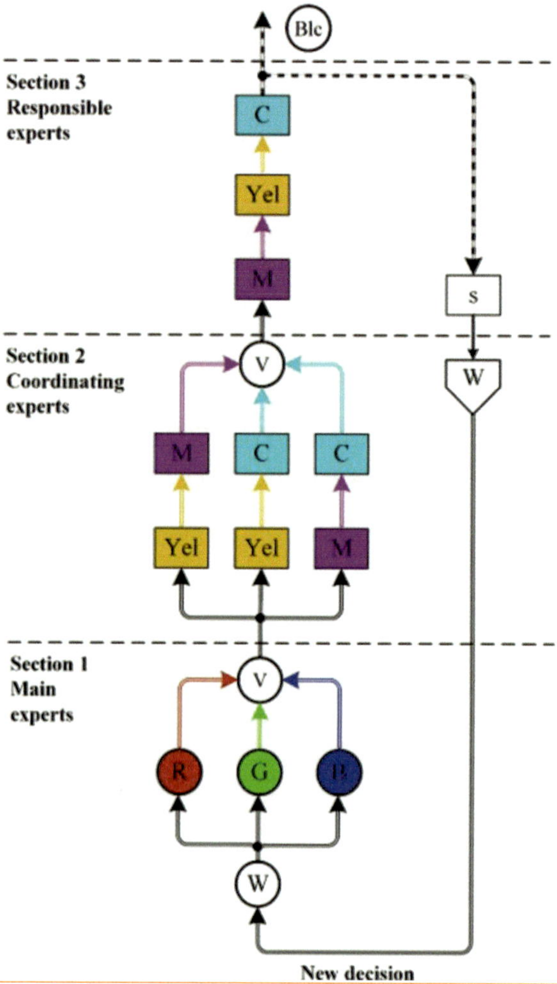

strongly support this decision. Thus, taking into account the above reasoning, the optical structure of the base coloroid is formed, shown in Figure 1.6.

The first logical operation of disjunction is written in the form of the sum of diagonal matrices

$$diag\,(R,\ 0,\ 0) + diag\,(0,\ G,\ 0) + diag\,(0,\ 0,\ B) = diag\,(R, G,\ B)\,.$$

Logical operations in the second section will take the form

$$diag\,(R, G,\ B) \times diag\,(R,\ G,\ 0) \times diag\,(R,\ 0,\ B) = diag\,(R,\ 0,\ 0)\,,$$

$$diag\,(R, G,\ B) \times diag\,(R,\ G,\ 0) \times diag\,(0,\ G,\ B) = diag\,(0, G,\ 0)\,,$$

$$diag\,(R, G,\ B) \times diag\,(R,\ 0,\ B) \times diag\,(0,\ G,\ B) = diag\,(0,\ 0, B)\,.$$

At the output of the second section, a disjunction operation is performed

$$diag\,(R,\ 0,\ 0) + diag\,(0,\ G,\ 0) + diag\,(0,\ 0,\ B) = diag\,(R, G,\ B)\,.$$

The third section forms the final solution

$$diag\,(R, G,\ B) \times diag\,(0,\ G,\ B) \times diag\,(R, G,\ 0) \times diag\,(R,\ 0,\ B)$$
$$= diag\,(0,\ 0,\ 0)\,.$$

1.5.2 Optical structures of different types of logical coloroids

Next, we consider the optical structures of various types of logical coloroids for the implementation of various components of the decision support system (DSS). (Please note that, for clarity, in the following text we use a more simplified view of the image of the light guides.)

The optical scheme (Figure 1.7) [34] assumes separate output of conventional decisions of the type "absolutely safe" $\{B, B, B\}$ or "absolutely dangerous" $\{R, R. R\}$ and includes a blocking circuit BC and a switching unit CB, including normally closed and open contacts, the main output channel Bl is blocked and interrupted, and the corresponding decision $\{B\}$, $\{R\}$ is output as the final one. In the case of output quanta $\{M\}$ or $\{W\}$, the light radiation passes simultaneously through two channels, CB does not work, and for output quanta $\{G\}$, the light radiation is blocked at the input of the light filter $\{M\}$ of the blocking circuit BC, thus, the main channel is not blocked and the output process continues.

Some decision-making problems do not include blocking decisions at the lower hierarchical levels, expanding the alternatives of different initial estimates (Figure 1.8).

An important type of operation in DSS problems is the blocking solution (BD), implemented by an optical scheme (Figure 1.9) and having strictly fixed filter values **Yel, C, M** and blocking of light radiation for any type of input color quanta of information.

Figure 1.7: Optical design of a coloroid with inference of an ordinary decision.

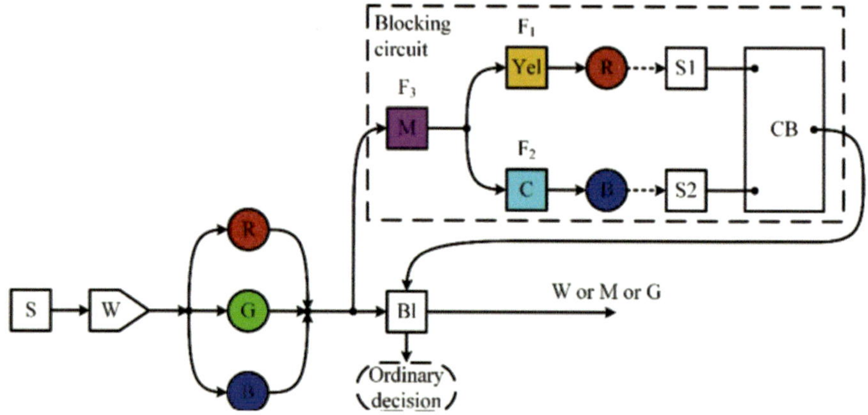

Figure 1.8: Optical design of a single-channel coloroid (9 input quantum).

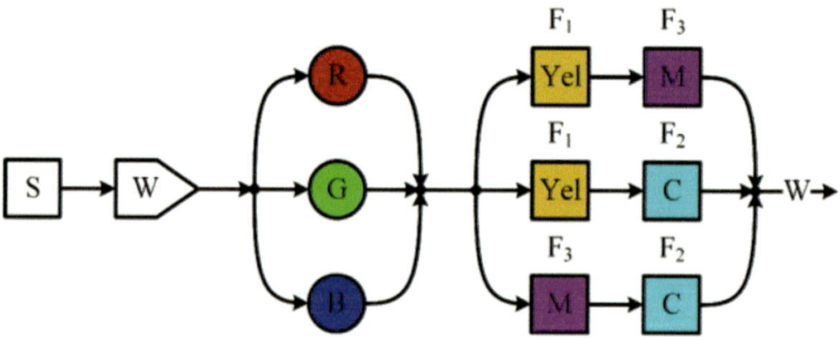

The generation of a new solution is realized by switching on the white light source S (Figure 1.10) both at the initial start of the logical inference process and for the trigger in the case of the absence of a solution $\{Blc\}$ in the output quantum. In this case, in response to the absence of light in the light guide, a new solution is generated, and the white light source S is switched on again.

The negation operation is a more complex logical action, since the negative solution is based on the absolutely opposite change of the original solution. The optical scheme (Figure 1.11) of the coloroid with an extended negation function for pairs ($\{W\}$, $\{Blc\}$ and $\{B\}$, $\{R\}$) includes light filters with fixed values F1–F5; Gate 1, Gate 2, Gate 3; light sources with switching on in the absence of light S1L1, S2L2, S3L3; blocking devices Bl1, Bl2.

Figure 1.9: Optical design of blocking coloroid (for input quantum {C}).

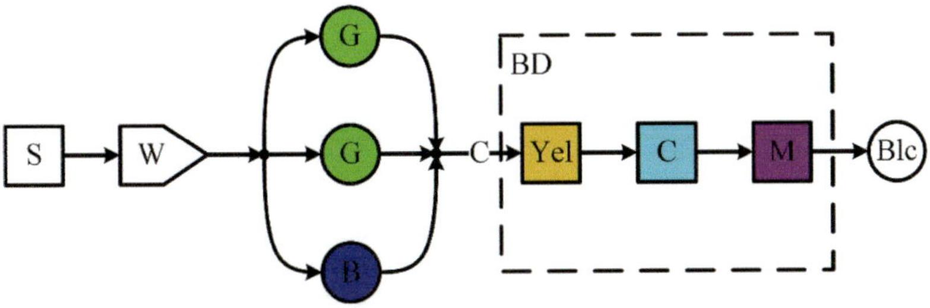

Figure 1.10: Optical scheme for generating a new solution (for input quanta {M}).

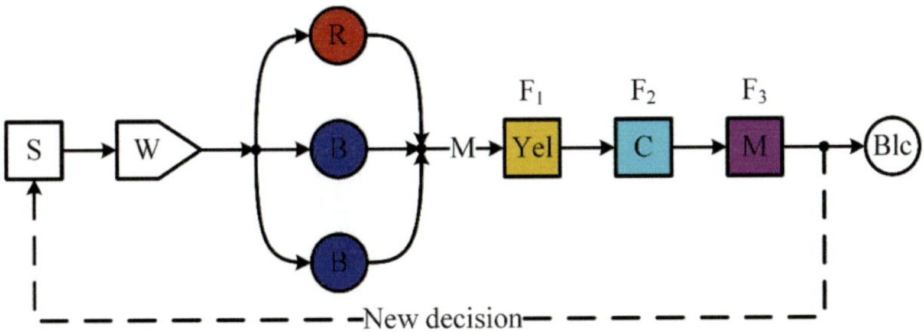

Switching and blocking of the corresponding blocks [33, 35] allows implementing logical negation operations of the type

$$\{Blc\} = \neg\{W\}, \{W\} = \neg\{Blc\},$$

$$\{R\} = \neg\{B\}, \neg\{R\} = \{B\}.$$

Let us consider the implementation of the logical operation NOT-OR (NOR) for an additive coloroid with a negation function for the output quantum of information $\{W\}$ with blocking of quanta $\{G\}$, $\{M\}$ based on the introduction of an additional optical circuit BC2 with fixed filters $\{R\}$, $\{G\}$, $\{B\}$ and the corresponding contact group CB (Figure 1.12).

The logical operation NOT–AND (NAND) is implemented by the optical circuit (Figure 1.13) for the intermediate output quantum $\{W\}$ by the operation of negation in the final output quantum $\{Blc\}$.

The hybrid fuzzy color optical scheme (Figure 1.14) allows us to bypass the idempotence property of color transformation and perform logical operations of algebraic addition and multiplication for two fuzzy sets A(x) and Q(x),

Figure 1.11: Optical scheme of the negation coloroid.

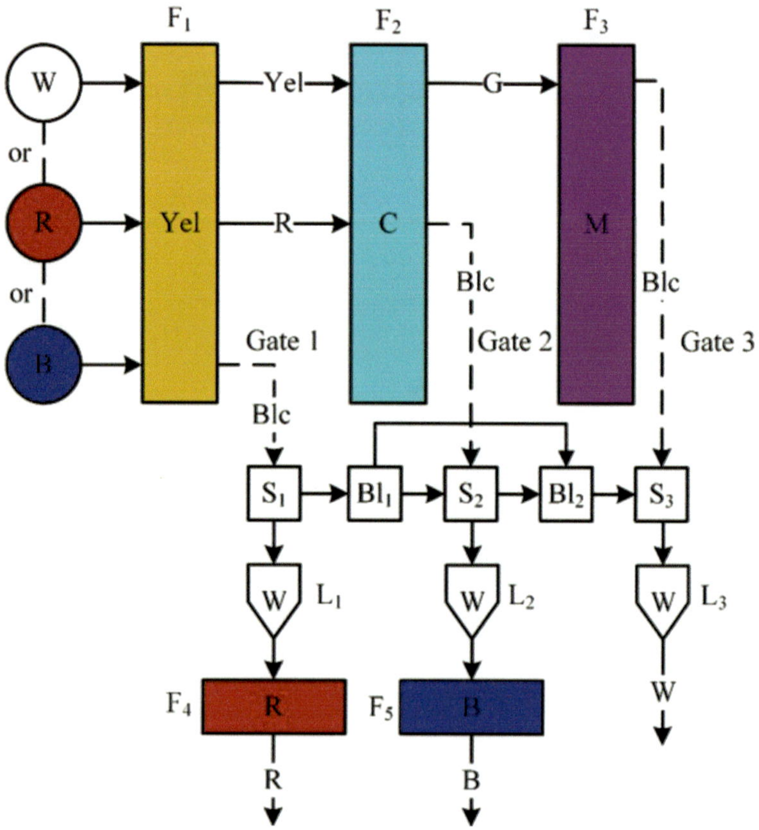

Figure 1.12: Optical circuit for implementing NOR logical operations.

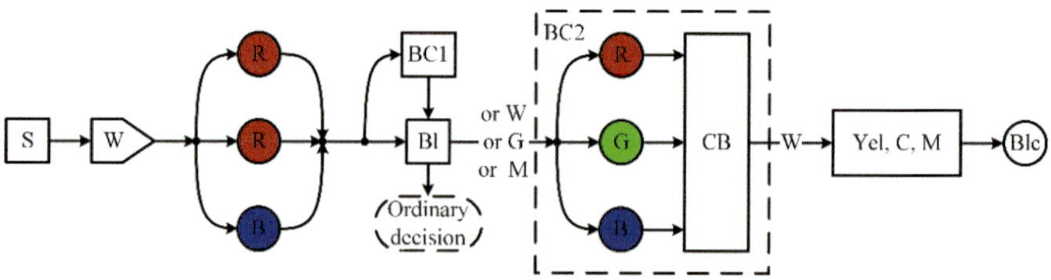

Figure 1.13: Optical circuit for implementing NAND logical operations.

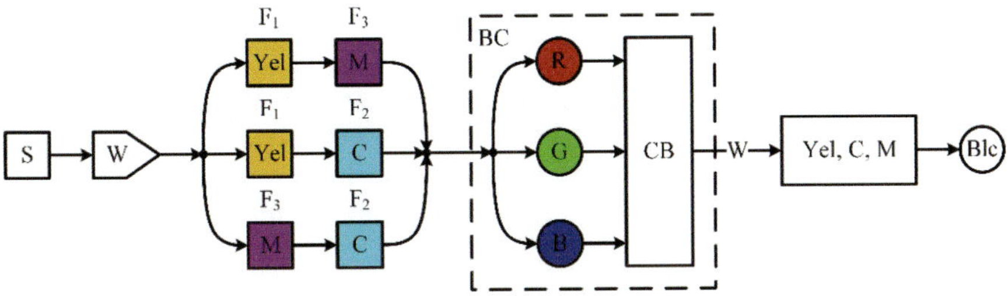

Figure 1.14: Hybrid coloroid structure.

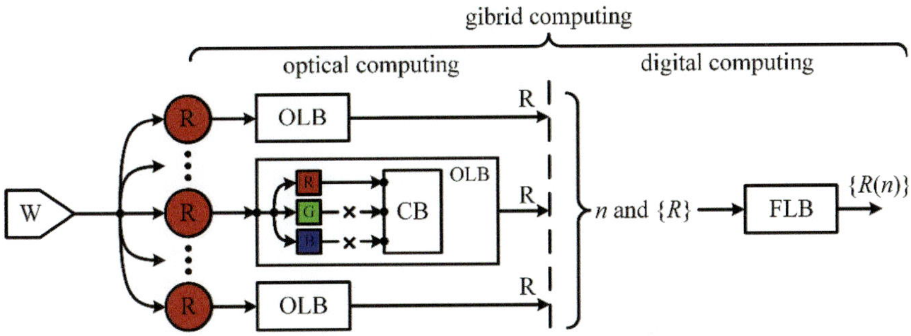

respectively, for membership functions μ, written in the form [1]

$$\mu_{A(+)Q}(x) = \mu_A(x) + \mu_Q(x) - \mu_A(x) \times \mu_Q(x),$$
$$\mu_{A(\times)Q}(x) = \mu_A(x) \times \mu_Q(x).$$

The accumulation of estimates changes the distribution of the membership function of the color fuzzy set and naturally only for solid estimates $\{R\}$ or $\{B\}$, since the rest have the property of "probability" and their accumulation will only strengthen this tendency [35].

The logical circuit is implemented in such a way that for an input signal of the form $\{Yel\}$, $\{M\}$, $\{C\}$ the output signal will simultaneously be in a combination of two light guides, for $\{W\}$ – three light guides, for $\{R\}$, $\{G\}$, $\{B\}$ – in the first, respectively the second or third. light guide. Then the information color quantum (excluding $\{G\}$) is allocated with the presence of light only in one light guide. The switching contact block (CB) implements a circuit for determining the corresponding color $\{R\}$ or $\{B\}$, as well as the number n of repeating channels and switches the information processing and logical output system to the digital fuzzy logic block (NLB).

Optical circuits of the type [22] allow the transformation of letters (Table 1.2) of the color coding of the alphabet into a binary code using a coloroid, which includes three parallel light channels and filters **Yel**, **M**, **C**, as well as the corresponding contact blocks (Figure 1.15, for example, for the letter "L" $\rightarrow \{B, R, G\}$).

Figure 1.15: Structural schemes for encoding letters (CB1–CB3 – contact blocks).

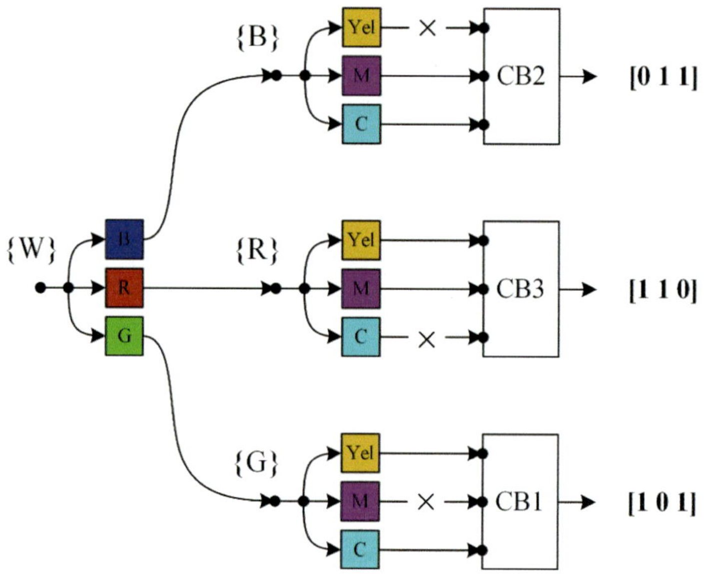

1.5.3 Optical architecture of logical color networks

The synthesis of multicomponent multilevel DSS involves, depending on the purpose of a specific technological task with large input fuzzy data, the formation of hierarchically organized structures of various types of logical inference rules and further implementation based on the proposed elementary, basic and other types of logical coroids.

To implement multi-level logical color networks of decision making, optical circuits with 45, 144 (Figures 1.16, 1.17) or more input fuzzy information quanta are used. The result of logical inference in computing networks assumes seven variants of possible solutions in relation to the goal of the task:

Figure 1.16: An example of the implementation of logical operations for a two-level coloroid.

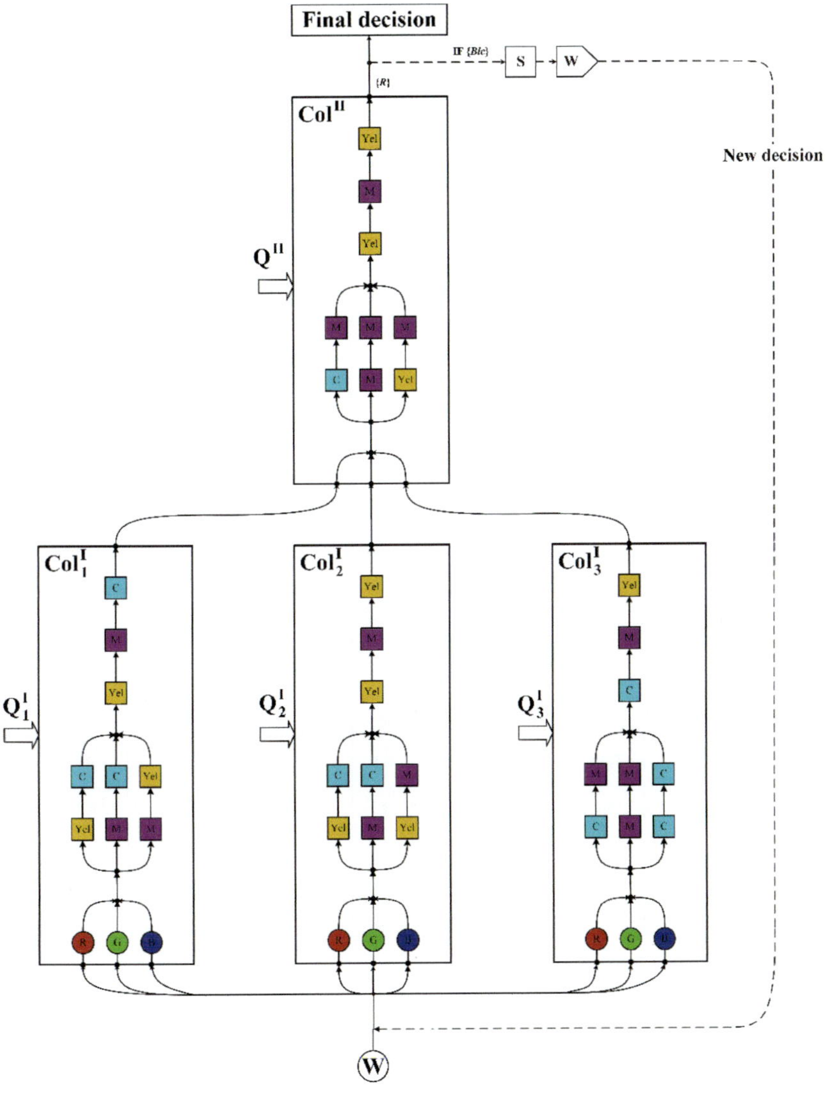

Figure 1.17: Coloroid's network.

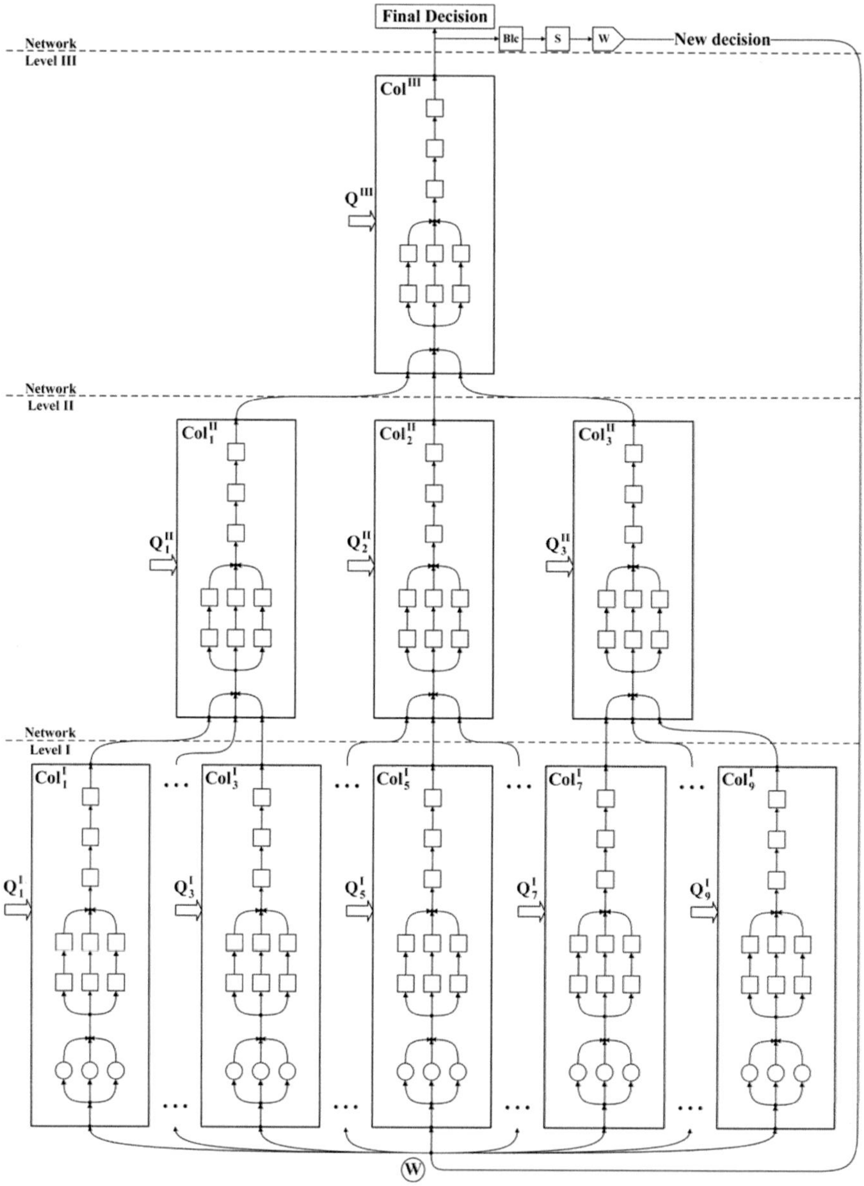

- "No decision", **Blc**, which results in a generation (**W**) of a new possible decision – based on input data changing in the process of decision search operations.
- "No – no positive decision" based on the overall assessment **R**.
- "Very probably no – very probably no positive decision", **Yel**.
- "Probably no – probably no positive decision", **M**.
- "Probably yes – probably a positive decision", **G**.
- "Very probably yes – very probably a positive decision", **C**.
- "Yes – a positive decision", **B**.

Let us give an example of a sequence of logical operations for a hieratical two-level coloroid network (left branch of the first level):

I. Hieratical network

Coloroid Col_1^I,

for input set $diag\,(R,\ 0,\ 0) + diag\,(0,\ G,\ 0) + diag\,(0,\ 0,\ B) = diag\,(R, G,\ B) = \{W\}$;

filters {*Yel,C*}:

$$diag\,(R, G,\ B) \times diag\,(R,\ G,\ 0) \times diag\,(0,\ G,\ B) = diag\,(0,\ G,\ 0)\,;$$

filters {*M, C*}:

$$diag\,(R, G,\ B) \times diag\,(R,\ 0,\ B) \times diag\,(0,\ G,\ B) = diag\,(0,\ 0,\ B)\,;$$

filters {*M,Yel*}:

$$diag\,(R, G,\ B) \times diag\,(R,\ 0,\ B) \times diag\,(R,\ G,\ 0) = diag\,(R,\ 0, 0)\,.$$

Disjunction:

$$diag\,(R,\ 0,\ 0) + diag\,(0,\ G,\ 0) + diag\,(0,\ 0,\ B) = diag\,(R, G,\ B) = \{W\}\,;$$

filters {*Yel,M,C*}:

$$diag\,(R, G,\ B) \times diag\,(R,\ G,\ 0) \times diag\,(R,\ 0,\ B) \times diag\,(0,\ G,\ B)$$
$$= diag\,(0,\ 0,\ 0)\,.$$

Coloroid Col_2^I,

for input set

$$diag\,(R,\ 0,\ 0) + diag\,(0,\ 0,\ B) + diag\,(0,\ 0,\ B)$$
$$= diag\,(R, 0,\ B) = \{M\}\,;$$

filters {*Yel,C*}:

$$diag\,(R, 0,\ B) \times diag\,(R,\ G,\ 0) \times diag\,(0,\ G,\ B)$$
$$= diag\,(0,\ 0,\ 0)\,;$$

filters {*M,C*}:

$$diag\,(R, 0,\ B) \times diag\,(R, 0,\ B) \times diag\,(0,\ G,\ B) = diag\,(0,\ 0,\ B)\,;$$

filters {*Yel,M*}:

$$diag\,(R, 0,\ B) \times diag\,(R, G,\ 0) \times diag\,(R, 0,\ B) = diag\,(R,\ 0,\ 0)\,.$$

Disjunction

$$diag\,(0,\ 0,\ 0) + diag\,(0,\ 0,\ B) + diag\,(R,\ 0,\ 0) = diag\,(R, 0,\ B)\,;$$

filters {*Yel,M,Yel*}:

$$diag\,(R, 0,\ B) \times diag\,(R,\ G,\ 0) \times diag\,(R,\ 0,\ B) \times diag\,(R,\ G,\ 0)$$
$$= diag\,(R,\ 0,\ 0)\,.$$

Coloroid Col_3^I,

for input set

$$diag\,(0, G,\ 0) + diag\,(0,\ 0,\ B) + diag\,(R,\ 0,\ B) = diag\,(0,\ 0,\ B)\,;$$

filters {*C,M*}:

$$diag\,(0,\ 0,\ B) \times diag\,(0,\ G,\ B) \times diag\,(R,\ 0,\ B) = diag\,(0,\ 0,\ B)\,;$$

filters {*M,M*}:

$$diag\,(0,\ 0,\ B) \times diag\,(R,\ 0,\ B) \times diag\,(R,\ 0,\ B) = diag\,(0,\ 0,\ B)\,;$$

filters {*C,C*}:

$$diag\,(0,\ 0,\ B) \times diag\,(0,\ G,\ B) \times diag\,(0, G,\ B) = diag\,(0,\ 0,\ B)\,.$$

Disjunction:

$$diag\,(0,\ 0,\ B) + diag\,(0,\ 0,\ B) + diag\,(0,\ 0,\ B) = diag\,(0,\ 0,\ B)\,;$$

filters {*C,M,Yel*}:

$$diag\,(0,\ 0,\ B) \times diag\,(0,\ G, B) \times diag\,(R,\ 0,\ B) \times diag\,(R,\ G,\ 0)$$
$$= diag\,(0,\ 0,\ 0)\,.$$

II. Hieratical network Coloroid Col$^{\text{II}}_{,}$ for input set:

$$diag\,(0,\ 0,\ 0) + diag\,(R,\ 0,\ 0) + diag\,(0,\ 0,\ B) = diag\,(R,\ 0,\ 0)\,;$$

filters {*C,M*}:

$$diag\,(R, 0,\ 0) \times diag\,(0,\ G,\ B) \times diag\,(R, 0,\ B) = diag\,(0,\ 0,\ 0)\,;$$

filters {*M,M*}:

$$diag\,(R, 0,\ 0) \times diag\,(R, 0,\ B) \times diag\,(R, 0,\ B) = diag\,(R,\ 0,\ 0)\,;$$

filters {*Yel,M*}:

$$diag\,(R, 0,\ 0) \times diag\,(R, G,\ B) \times diag\,(R, 0,\ B) = diag\,(R,\ 0,\ 0)\,.$$

Disjunction

$$diag\,(0,\ 0,\ 0) + diag\,(R,\ 0,\ 0) + diag\,(R,\ 0,\ 0) = diag\,(R,\ 0,\ 0)\,;$$

filters {*Yel,M,Yel*}:

$$diag\,(R,\ 0,\ 0) \times diag\,(R,\ G,\ 0) \times diag\,(R,\ 0,\ B) \times diag\,(R,\ G,\ 0)$$
$$= diag\,(R,\ 0,\ 0)\,.$$

Final Decision – R.

1.6 Summary

We propose a systematic approach to the principles of constructing the structure and components of logical computing networks based on optical transformation of input fuzzy information in the form of color quanta (sets). We show that the formation of multicomponent hierarchically organized systems of logical decision inference is based mainly on two main logical operations of disjunction and conjunction. These operations are implemented by non-switchable logical components (coloroids). This ensures an extremely high speed of information processing. We present several equivalent mathematical models of color quanta of information based on logical operations, on truth operands, on diagonal matrices, and on fuzzy sets. We also show the implementation of basic operations.

To implement logical operations and decision support systems based on these operations, we describe the following optical logical devices: elementary additive and subtractive coloroids, an optimized base coloroid, as well as coloroids corresponding to negation, to NOR, to NAND, coloroids for the formation of a new solution and for blocking a solution, a coloroid for hybrid digital-fuzzy calculations, and a coloroid for digital encoding of color quanta.

The proposed structures of optical coloroids allow the formation of multi-level and multi-component hierarchically organized computing networks for decision support systems in various information problems with large fuzzy databases.

References

[1] L. Zadeh, 'The role of fuzzy logic in modelling, identification and control,' Modelling 15 (3): 191–203, 1994. DOI:10.4173/mic.1994.3.9

[2] V. Kreinovich (ed.), 'Uncertainty Modeling,' Springer Verlag, Cham, Switzerland, 2017.

[3] V.M. Kuntsevich, Synthesis of Robust Optimal Adaptive Control Systems for Nonstationary Objects under Bounded Disturbances, Journal of Automation and Information Sciences, NY, Begell house inc., Vol. 36, Issue 3, pp. 14 – 24, 2004. DOI:~10.1615/JAutomatInfScien.v36.i3.20

[4] V.L. Timchenko, Y.P. Kondratenko, 'Robust stabilization of Marine Mobile Objects on the Basis of Systems with Variable Structure of Feedbacks,' Journal of Automation and Information Sciences, Vol. 43, No. 6, New York: Begel House Inc., pp. 16-29, 2011. DOI:10.1615/JAutomatInfScien.v43.i6.20

[5] V.L. Timchenko, D.O. Lebedev, 'Optimization of Processes of Robust Control of Quadcopter for Monitoring of Sea Waters,' Journal of Automation and Information Sciences, New York, Begell house inc., Vol. 51, Is. 2, pp. 1 – 10, 2019. DOI:~10.1615/JAutomatInfScien.v51.i2.10

[6] V.L. Timchenko, D. Lebedev, 'Algorithmic Procedures Synthesis of Robust-Optimal Control for Moving Objects,' in: Y.P. Kondratenko, V.M. Kuntsevich, A.A. Chikrii, V.F. Gubarev (Eds.), Recent Developments in Automatic Control Systems, River Publishers, Gistrup, pp. 289-323, 2022. https://www.scopus.com/pages/publications/85149376557

[7] V. L. Timchenko, V. Horbov, 'Robust Stabilization of an Autonomous Marine Vehicle on Programmed Trajectories,' Proceedings of the 7th IEEE International Conference on Methods and Systems of Navigation

and Motion Control (MSNMC), pp. 101-105, 2023. DOI:10.1109/MSNMC61017.2023.10329125

[8] C. Cole, 'Optical and electrical programmable computing energy use comparison,' Optics Express, Vol. 29, Issue 9, pp. 13153-13170, 2021. DOI:~10.1364/OE.420027

[9] P. L. McMahon, 'The physics of optical computing,' Nat Rev Phys 5, pp. 717–734, 2023. https://doi.org/10.1038/s42254-023-00645-5

[10] M. Matuszewski, A. Prystupiuk, A. Opala, 'The role of all-optical neural networks,' arXiv:2306.06632v2, [cs.ET] 13 Jun 2023. https://doi.org/10.48550/arXiv.2306.06632

[11] Y.J. Jung, S. Yu, S. Koo, et al., 'Reconfigurable all-optical logic AND, NAND, OR, NOR, XOR and XNOR by photonic crystal nonlinear cavities,' Conference on Lasers and Electro-Optics, Pacific Rim, paper TuB4_3, 2009. DOI:10.1109/CLEOPR.2009.5292059.

[12] S. Ma, Z. Chen, N.K. Dutta, 'All-optical logic gates based on two-photon absorption in semiconductor optical amplifiers,' Optics Communications 282 (23): 4508-4512, 2009. https://doi.org/10.1016/j.optcom.2009.08.039

[13] V. Jandieri, R. Khomeriki, T. Onoprishvili, et al., 'Functional all-optical logic gates for true time-domain signal processing in nonlinear photonic crystal waveguides,' Optics Express 28(12): 18317-18331, 2020. DOI:~10.1364/OE.395015

[14] T. Kawano, 'Printable Optical Logic Gates with CIELAB Color Coding System for Boolean,' Operation-Mediated Handling of Colors Genetic and Evolutionary Computing (ICGEC), IEEE, pp. 270-275, 2012. DOI: 10.1109/ICGEC.2012.121.

[15] X. Wang, H. Fei, H. Lin, et al., 'High-performance spiral all-optical logic gate based on topological edge states of valley photonic crystal,' arXiv:2209.08358 [physics.optics] 2022. https://doi.org/10.48550/arXiv.2209.08358

[16] L. P. Caballero, M. L. Povinelli, J. C. Ramirez, et al., 'Photonic crystal integrated logic gates and circuits,' Optics Express 30(2): 1976-1993, 2022. https://doi.org/10.1364/OE.444714

[17] Z. Zhu, J. Yuan, L. Jiang, 'Multifunctional and multichannels all-optical logic gates based on the in-plane coherent control of localized surface plasmons,' Optics Letters 45(23), pp. 6362-6365, 2020. https://doi.org/10.1364/OL.402085

[18] V. Timchenko, V. Kreinovich, Y. Kondratenko, 'Logical platforms for mobile application in decision support systems based on color information processing,' Journal of Mobile Multimedia, vol. 20, no. 3, pp. 679–698, 2024, https://doi.org/10.13052/jmm1550-4646.2037

[19] S.R. Ahmed, R. Baghdadi, M. Bernadskiy, et al., 'Universal photonic artificial intelligence acceleration,' Nature, Vol. 640, pp. 368-374, 2025, https://doi.org/10.1038/s41586-025-08854-x

[20] A. Palivela, 'Photonic computing takes a step toward fruition,' Physics, 18, 84, 2025, https://physics.aps.org/articles/v18/84

[21] A. Lupo, O. Kosheleva, V. Kreinovich, V. Timchenko, Y. Kondratenko, 'There is still plenty of room at the bottom: Feynman's vision of quantum computing 65 years later,' in: Y.P. Kondratenko, A.I. Shevchenko (eds) Research Tendencies and Prospect Domains for AI Development and Implementation, River Publishers, 2024, pp. 77–86. https://www.scopus.com/pages/publications/85202986959

[22] V. Timchenko, V. Kreinovich, Yu. Kondratenko, 'Color optical computing: visualization, numbers, alphabet,' CEUR Workshop Proceedings, Vol. 3790, pp. 123-132, 2024, https://ceur-ws.org/Vol-3790/paper11.pdf

[23] Z. K. Moritaka, T. Kawano, 'Spectroscopic analysis of the model color filters used for computation of CIELAB-based optical logic gates,' ICIC Express Letters, Part B: Applications 5(6), pp. 1715-1720, 2014.

[24] N. Ohta, A.R. Robertson, 'Colorimetry. Fundamentals and Applications,' J. Wiley&Sons, 2005.

[25] M. Ebner, 'Color Constancy,' J. Wiley&Sons, 2007.

[26] A. Koshan, M. Abidi, 'Digital Color Image Processing,' J. Wiley&Sons, 2008.

[27] N. Sugano, 'Fuzzy Set Theoretical Approach to the Tone Triangle System,' International Journal of Software Science and Computational Intelligence, 5(3), pp. 33-54, 2015. DOI:10.4018/ijssci.2013070103

[28] S. Kato, I. Shinomiya, F. Mori, N. Sugano, 'Fuzzy Set Theoretical Analysis of Human Membership Values on the Color Triangle,' Pattern Recognition Applications and Methods, pp. 239-246, 2014. DOI:10.5220/0004826502390246

[29] V. Timchenko, Yu. Kondratenko, V. Kreinovich, 'Why Color Optical Computing?,' In: N.H. Phuong, V. Kreinovich (eds) Deep Learning and Other Soft Computing Techniques. Studies in Computational Intelligence, vol. 1097, pp. 227-233, 2023, Springer, Cham, https://doi.org/10.1007/978-3-031-29447-1_20

[30] V. Timchenko, Yu. Kondratenko, V. Kreinovich, 'Interval-Valued and Set-Valued Extensions of Discrete Fuzzy Logics, Belnap Logic, and Color Optical Computing,' in: S. Massanet, et al. (eds) Fuzzy Logic and Technology, and Aggregation Operators, EUSFLAT AGOP 2023, Lecture Notes in Computer Science, Vol. 14069. Springer, Cham, 2023, pp. 297–303. https://doi.org/10.1007/978-3-031-39965-7_25

[31] V. Timchenko, Yu. Kondratenko, V. Kreinovich, 'Decision support system for the safety of ship navigation based on optical color logic gates,' CEUR Workshop Proceedings, Vol. 3347, pp. 42-52, 2022. https://ceur-ws.org/Vol-3347/Paper_4.pdf

[32] V. Timchenko, Yu. Kondratenko, O. Kozlov, V. Kreinovich, 'Fuzzy color computing based on optical logical architecture,' in: Kahraman, C., et al. (eds) Intelligent and Fuzzy Systems, INFUS 2023, Lecture Notes in Networks and Systems, vol. 758, pp. 491–498, 2023, Springer, Cham, https://doi.org/10.1007/978-3-031-39774-5_55

[33] V. Timchenko, Yu. Kondratenko, V. Kreinovich, 'The Architecture of Optical Logical Coloroid with Fuzzy Computing,' CEUR Workshop Proceedings, Vol. 3373, pp. 638-648, 2023, https://ceur-ws.org/Vol-3373/paper44.pdf

[34] V. Timchenko, Yu. Kondratenko, V. Kreinovich, 'Implementation of Optical Logic Gates Based on Color Filters,' in: Z. Hu, I. Dychka, M. He (eds) Advances in Computer Science for Engineering and Education VI, ICCSEEA 2023, Lecture Notes on Data Engineering and Communications Technologies, vol 181, pp. 126–136, 2023, Springer, Cham. https://doi.org/10.1007/978-3-031-36118-0_12

[35] V. Timchenko, V. Kreinovich, Y. Kondratenko, V. Horbov V. 'Hybrid Fuzzy-Color Computing Based on Optical Logical Architecture,' in: C. Kahraman, et al. (eds) Intelligent and Fuzzy Systems, INFUS 2024, Lecture Notes in Networks and Systems, vol 1090, pp. 266–274, 2024, Springer, Cham. https://doi.org/10.1007/978-3-031-67192-0_33

CHAPTER

2

Optical Color Computing Architecture in Decision Support Systems

V. Timchenko[1], V. Kreinovich[2], Y. Kondratenko[3,4], and O. Iegorov[5]

[1]Admiral Makarov National University of Shipbuilding, Mykolaiv, Ukraine
[2]Department of Computer Science, University of Texas at El Paso, El Paso, TX, USA
[3]Intelligent Information Systems Department, Petro Mohyla Black Sea National University, Mykolaiv, Ukraine
[4]Institute of Artificial Intelligence Problems, Kyiv, Ukraine
[5]Admiral Makarov National University of Shipbuilding, Mykolaiv, Ukraine
Email: vl.timchenko58@gmail.com, vladik@utep.edu, y_kondrat2002@yahoo.com, alex.yegorov@gmail.com

Abstract

In this chapter, we carry out a comparative analysis of the efficiency of optical color logic devices in processing fuzzy input information in comparison with various algorithms (FPGA, x86-x64, ARM, ARM serial execution) based on the binary representation of fuzzy sets. To implement the proposed optical architecture for constructing a decision support system (DSS), we describe the principles of forming a real-time changing multifactorial fuzzy color database. These principles are illustrated on the example of components of a dispatch service for managing intensive traffic of sea ships and/or aircraft. We present examples of implementing components of a two-level DSS for traffic safety management and for organizing servicing of sea vessels and aircraft. The results

DOI: 10.1201/9788743810322-2

of the performance evaluation of computational operations with fuzzy sets demonstrate a higher speed of optical computations due to a significantly smaller number of operations and the organization of parallel structures. We also provide examples of using logical operations in DSS to obtain estimates for a certain set of input data. These examples show the effectiveness of the proposed approach.

Keywords: Efficiency, decision support system, fuzzy optical coloroid, safety, ship, aircraft, medical solutions

2.1 Efficiency of Optical Color Computing

The use of optical color computing architecture in decision support systems for technological systems with very big fuzzy input data has the following advantages:

- Higher computational efficiency
- Expansion of structural capabilities for parallel processing of arrays of input information
- Low hardware costs of used energy.

These advantages, in comparison to the use of traditional semiconductor-based architectures, was shown in [1–3]. In this chapter, we continue this comparison; namely, we compare the structural features of computational algorithmic procedures of optical color computing with the most efficient binary semiconductor processors.

2.1.1 Review of popular CPU architectures

In today's computing landscape, central processing unit (CPU) architectures are at the forefront to support the performance and efficiency of a variety of applications ranging from consumer services (e.g., mobile electronics) to mission-critical systems (e.g., healthcare and medicine). In this section, we briefly review three popular *CPU* architectures [4], *x86-64*, *ARM*, and *FPGA*, and we evaluate the advantages of each architecture in processing fuzzy logic data for decision support systems (DSS).

The x86-64 architecture has evolved from its 32-bit predecessor by expanding the instruction set to 64-bit processing – to support larger memory addresses and to provide more efficient data processing. The 64-bit enhancement has significantly increased the computational capabilities by increasing the number of available registers (sixteen additional 64-bit general-purpose registers). SIMD instructions such as MMX, SSE, and AVX enable parallel data processing, making the architecture more suitable for tasks such as fuzzy logic computations in DSS. The architecture supports up to 16 parallel integer or floating-point operations using XMM registers.

The ARM (Advanced RISC Machine) architecture is distinguished by its power-efficient design, which has solidified its prominence across mobile, embedded, and high-performance computing domains. ARM processors are predicated on a reduced instruction set computing (RISC) paradigm, which streamlines instruction execution, minimizes cycle complexity, and maximizes computational throughput.

ARM's adherence to the RISC architecture emphasizes streamlined instruction cycles and minimal hardware complexity. By reducing instruction set intricacy, ARM processors achieve superior performance per watt compared to conventional complex instruction set computing (CISC) architectures such as x86-64.

As data processing requirements piled, ARM developed extensions to support single instruction, multiple data (SIMD) capabilities, this way facilitating concurrent processing for computationally intensive tasks such as image recognition and real-time analytics. This functionality was designed to match Intel's SSE and AVX extensions found in the x86-64 architecture.

The field-programmable gate array (FPGA) architecture represents a flexible and reconfigurable hardware platform capable of executing parallel computations with high efficiency. FPGAs evolved from programmable logic arrays (PLAs) and complex programmable logic devices (CPLDs). PLAs implemented simple logic functions using programmable AND–OR matrices, while CPLDs introduced interconnection matrices and macro cells, laying the groundwork for FPGA architectures.

Its key characteristics, for our purpose, are parallel processing capability and high-speed data processing.

Parallel processing capability is particularly advantageous for computationally intensive operations like the use of fuzzy logic in decision support systems. This is achieved by extensive parallelization through customizable logic blocks, enabling concurrent execution of multiple tasks.

Modern FPGAs integrate specialized logic elements, including DSP blocks and hardware accelerators, to achieve high-speed data processing.

2.1.2 Peculiarities of algorithm execution on popular CPU platforms

Fuzzy logic processing normally requires using complex algorithms. These algorithms include various logical operations, e.g. fuzzy analogues of AND, OR, NOT, XOR, etc.

Each CPU platform has its own architecture, it was created at different times and had specific design choices made during its evolution. This explains some differences present in their capabilities of data processing [5], namely in their approach to perform logical operations. We will only mention the most important and computationally meaningful advantages in this section.

The x86-64 architecture is distinguished by reliable single-thread performance and mature SIMD (single instruction, multiple data) functionality. Modern x86-64 central processing units (CPUs), frequently operating between 3 and 5GHz, can issue multiple instructions per clock cycle. These processors integrate robust vectorization tools, such as SSE (streaming SIMD extensions) and AVX (advanced vector extensions), enabling efficient execution of bitwise tasks (e.g., AND, OR, or NOT). Owing to its extensive software ecosystem, x86-64 remains well-suited for server workloads and desktop applications, including cryptography and data-intensive processes. In high-performance computing contexts, x86-64 leverages SIMD acceleration and strong parallelization capabilities.

The ARM platform, on the other hand, is well known for energy efficiency and multicore design scalability being prioritized. Based on RISC (reduced instruction set computing) principles, ARM processors aim to reduce power consumption per instruction. Such ARM extensions as NEON (ARM's SIMD extension) or SVE (scalable vector extension) are capable of parallel execution of bitwise operations, which results in enhanced throughput. Its systems find wide adoption in embedded and mobile areas. IoT (Internet of Things) devices, where stringent power constraints dictate system design, is one of these application areas. Another application area is mobile platforms, such as smartphones, which benefit from ARM's capacity to handle moderate logical computations under limited resource constraints.

Speaking of FPGAs, their sweet spot is explained by flexibility in hardware-level parallelism. Each device contains numerous LUT (look-up table) elements and intricate interconnects. This facilitates concurrent execution of considerable sets of bitwise operations. Given a careful and well-thought through design pipeline, these computations can be completed in near-one-cycle time. FPGAs also lead to reduced energy usage per operation. This is achieved by using customized hardware descriptions. Given these advantages, FPGAs are frequently employed as specialized accelerators for tasks like signal processing,

AI (artificial intelligence) inference, and cryptography (especially in domains requiring deterministic and high-throughput behavior).

As a result, we can think of x86-64 as a strong candidate for general purpose servers and high-performance computing tasks. ARM is energy efficient and multicore scalable, mobile, IoT, and edge-based favorite. FPGA stands out in delivering advanced parallel processing and configurable hardware acceleration, which is especially advantageous for real-time operations.

2.1.3 Estimation of the relative effectiveness of algorithmic operations by different architectures

Let us estimate the relative effectiveness of a sample set of algorithmic binary operations if run by coloroids vs by popular CPU architectures.

Considering the computational performance of the proposed optical architecture, the fundamental and currently open question is the manufacturability of the design devices. Based on fairly general assumptions about the physical implementation of optical fibers and light filters, their sizes, taking into account that these devices use the visible spectrum of light radiation, come from the fact that the color filter distance is within 3 μm. A three-level hierarchically organized coloroid network [6,7] in the longitudinal direction uses about 30 segments of light guides, so we assume the longitudinal size of the color network design is 100 μm. When calculating the speed of logical calculations, let us take into account that the transverse size does not matter, since the light beam, passing through a given configuration of light filters, moves mainly in the longitudinal direction. Thus, complete processing of input information, consisting of 144 logical operations of disjunction and conjunction, is carried out in a time interval determined by the ratio

$$\frac{\text{longitudinal size of the coloroid network}}{\text{speed of light (in vacuum)}} = \frac{100{*}10^{-6}\ \text{m}}{3{*}10^{8}\,\frac{\text{m}}{\text{s}}} \approx 3{*}10^{-13}\ \text{s}.$$

Thus, the entire given volume of information in the logical coloroid is processed in a time interval equivalent to three elementary binary computational operations.

One of the advantages of the proposed optical architecture is that when the hierarchy level of the logical structure increases (for example, to a four-level network – Figure 2.1) then, taking into account the parallelism of calculations, the number of input fuzzy quanta (as well as the number of computational operations) increases to 441, i.e. more than 3 times, while the longitudinal size

Figure 2.1: Four-level hierarchical network.

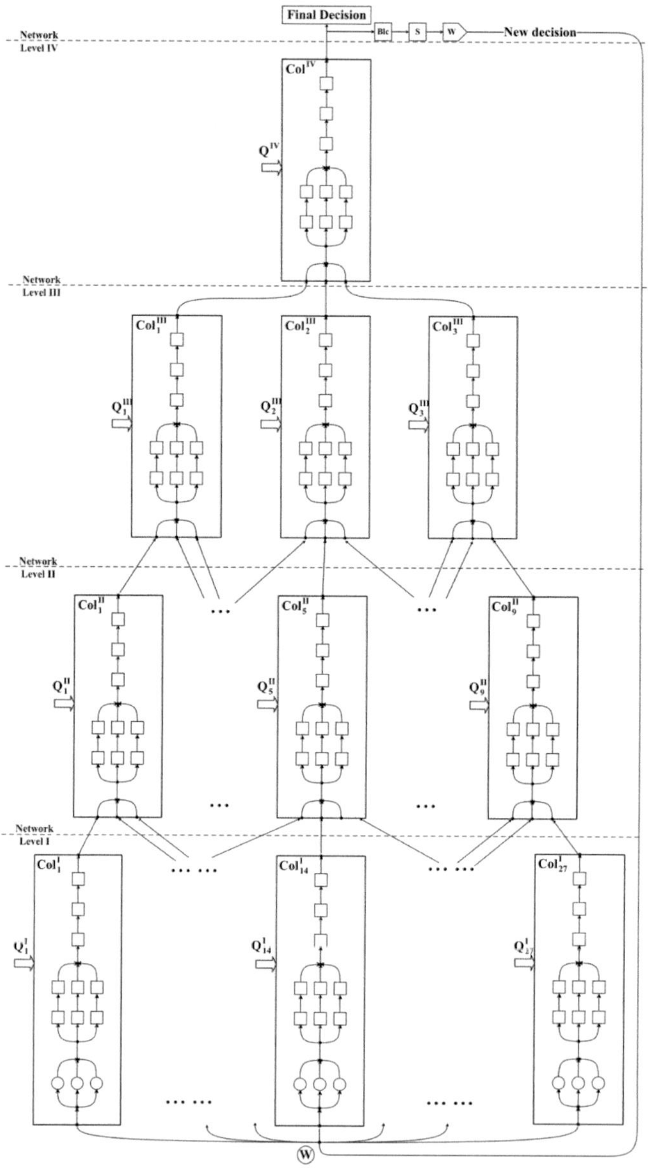

of the coloroid (approximately) will increase by only 30%. And a given volume of information in the logical coloroid is processed in a time interval equivalent to four binary computational operations.

Based on the information provided, we will determine the number of cycles required for popular CPU platforms to execute a basic coloroid algorithm. With this data, we can estimate the runtime (in seconds) of a three-level hierarchically organized coloroid network algorithm on those CPU platforms.

2.1.3.1 Number of CPU cycles per coloroid

Figure 2.2 shows the basic coloroid Col_1^I, with an optimized algorithmic structure for making a basic decision. It includes two elementary operations of disjunction and elementary operations of conjunction. There are also operations of initial assignment of input color information sets (for example, in

Figure 2.2: Operations within a base coloroid.

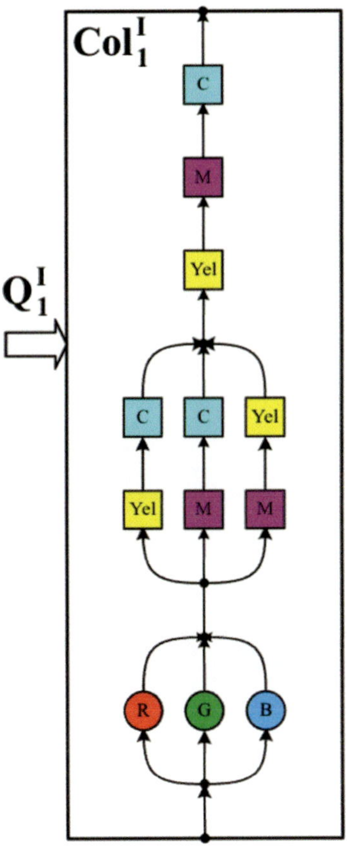

Figure 2.2, **R**, **B**, **G**) and subsequent logical processing in three parallel branches, and after the summation operation in one subtraction branch. The first composite operation is a conjunction for each of the three input signals. The second composite operation is a disjunction of three sets. The third composite operation is a conjunction in three parallel branches with combinations of two sets. The fourth composite operation is again a disjunction of three sets. The fifth composite operation is a conjunction of three sets.

The sequence and type of above operations, as well the number of cycles required to perform each (unification and intersection [6, 7]) operation respectively, are used to calculate a number of cycles to process the algorithm encoded in a basic coloroid.

In Table 2.1 calculation results are detailed (per operation, per number of sets, per number of parallel operations).

For a clearer comparison of the results, we summarize them in Table 2.2.

It is clear that coloroid used fewer cycles compared to FPGA, and much fewer compared to x86-64 or ARM-versions. Figure 2.3 visually presents this difference by using the logarithmic scale for the number of cycles.

Figure 2.3: Logarithmic chart for number of cycles needed for a single logarithmic operation.

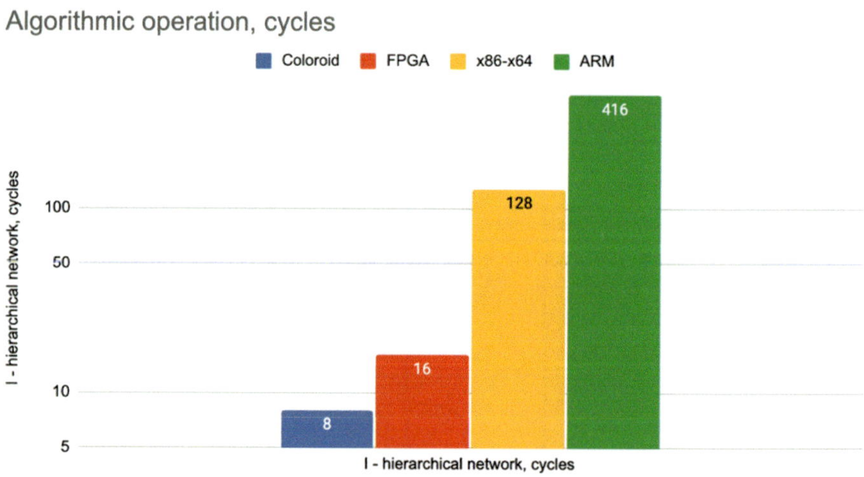

Coloroid-based computations demonstrate significantly fewer cycles compared to FPGA, x86-64, and ARM architectures, highlighting their efficiency

Table 2.1: Detailed calculation results for number of consumed cycles for a single algorithmic operation.

#	Description	Sets, count	Parallel ops, count	Total CPU cycles, count			
				Coloroid	FPGA	x86-x64	ARM
1	Conjunction of each copy against filter 1	2	3	1	3	24	78
2	Disjunction of initial values (3 sets)	3	1	1	2	16	52
3	Conjunction of each copy against filter 1	2	3	1	3	24	78
4	Conjunction of each copy against filter 2	2	3	1	3	24	78
5	Disjunction of twice filtered values	3	1	1	2	16	52
6	Filtering through filter 3	2	1	1	1	8	26
7	Filtering through filter 4	2	1	1	1	8	26
8	Filtering through filter 5	2	1	1	1	8	26
	Total cycles			8	16	128	416

Table 2.2: Detailed calculation results for number of consumed cycles for a single algorithmic operation.

Total number of consumed processing cycles			
Coloroid	FPGA	x86-x64	ARM
8	16	128	416

in implementing algorithmic binary operations. The analysis of hierarchical networks further emphasizes the advantages of parallelized logical operations within a basic coloroid structure.

2.1.3.2 CPU processing time comparison with coloroid DSS

In the previous section, we calculated the approximate number of cycles required to process the operations of the basic coloroid algorithm. The current section focuses on finding out the processing time for a three-level hierarchically organized coloroid network algorithm.

A three-level hierarchically organized coloroid network algorithm contains nine coloroids at the first level, three coloroids at the second level, and a single coloroid at the third level. The total coloroid count is 13.

Let us estimate how much time is needed to implement all these algorithmic operations on a usual CPU architecture. This is how we can come up with this estimate:

- First, we find the time (in seconds) that it takes to execute a single CPU cycle.
- Then, we multiple this time by the number of executing cycles per basic coloroid.
- After that, we multiple the resulting product by the number of coloroids.
- Finally, we divide the resulting time by number of cores for (x86 and for ARM) or by the number of ogical cells (FPGA).

This leads to the following formula:

$$T_{execution} = T_{cycle} \times N_{cycles} \times N_{algorithm\ ops\ run} / N_{cores/cells}$$

This formula is applied to all CPU-based processors, but, of course, not to the coloroid, because coloroid execution time is estimated based on the speed of light in vacuum and the coloroid's length. The results of these calculations are presented in Table 2.3.

Table 2.3: Full algorithm CPU processing times.

Processor	Frequency, 10^9 Hz	Cycle time T_{cycle}, 10^{-10} s	Cores/ Cells $N_{cores/c}$ count	Algorithm execution N_{cyc} cycles	Algorithm operation run $N_{algorithm}$ count	Execution time $T_{execution}$, 10^{-10} s
Coloroid	3300	N/A	N/A	8	13	0.003
FPGA	1.5	6.67	15360	16	13	0.09
x86-64	5.1	1.96	16	128	13	204
ARM	3.3	3.03	4	416	13	4096

For sample CPUs we have taken the top consumer level Intel Core Ultra 9 185H (x86-64) and Cortex-A76 (ARM) processors. For an FPGA, we took an enterprise level (both performance-wise and price-wise) Xilinx Virtex Ultra-Scale+ VU19P.

Note that a DSP slice [8] (local cell) in an FPGA is considered the smallest independent processing unit, akin to a CPU core in conventional processors. These slices handle arithmetic and logic operations and enable FPGAs to execute thousands of tasks in parallel.

Let's summarize the results from Table 2.3 into Table 2.4.

Table 2.4: Full algorithm – comparison execution times.

Device	Execution time, 10^{-10} s
Coloroid	0.003
FPGA	0.09
X86-64	204
ARM	4096

Figure 2.4 visually shows how faster a coloroid-based processor is in comparison with the usual CPU-based processors.

Figure 2.4: Full algorithm – execution time comparison.

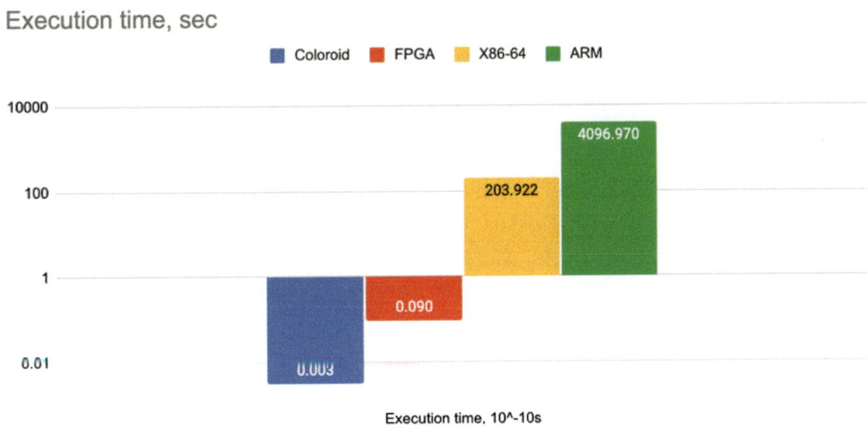

Evidently, coloroid device is approximately 10^7 times faster than an ARM processor, 10^5 times faster than an x86-64 one and 30 times faster than FPGA.

Although it may seem that FPGA-based processor processing time came relatively to coloroid – this processing time is achieved by paying a toll of a top-tier hardware with 15360 parallel processing units – which is currently priced around 100k USD. In addition, highly skilled programming personnel are required to develop optimized software circuit logic on the FPGAs.

2.2 Implementation of Optical Logical Color Architectures in Decision Support Systems

2.2.1 Principles of formation of fuzzy color databases

The proposed logical-optical color architecture involves the formation of a hierarchically structured database based on expert assessments or an array of sensory information about the functional task of the functioning of a technological system, including the processes of making management decisions.

First of all, it is necessary to determine the array of initial, most important input information, formed, for example, by the main experts who determine the purpose of the decision-making process.

The base coloroid underlying logical decision networks contains three input signals. The number of inputs signals to a single is limited by the logical property of idempotence – it is equal to the number of different basic colors [6, 7, 9–11]. Thus, to process n input signals, we need $k = n/3$ base coloroids. Such a structure of the first hierarchical level of the network necessitates $6{\star}k$ assessments of "coordinating" experts and k assessments of "responsible" experts, i.e. a total of $12{\star}k$ expert assessments. The logical network presented in the DSS (Figure 2.1) includes 27 input assessments of the ≪main≫ experts, 78 assessments of "coordinating" experts and 39 "responsible" experts. If it is possible for decision-making processes to exclude blocking assessments at the first and second hierarchical levels, there still remain 27 input assessments of the "main" experts, 78 assessments of "coordinating" experts and 3 "responsible" experts.

Based on the reasoning given, for example, in the works [10, 11], we will determine the ranking of the "main" expert assessments by fuzzy information quanta of the primary colors. The remaining assessments, "coordinating" and "responsible", are determined by fuzzy information quanta corresponding to additional colors.

Let us consider a database for assessing the safety of vessel traffic on a shipping channel, taking into account the simultaneous movement of *N* vessels with the corresponding safety level. Analysis of factors affecting the safety of traffic for the considered stage of vessel traffic (Table 2.5) will allow us to identify the most significant of them:

- The number of vessels simultaneously located on the most difficult sections of the channel
- The safety level of vessels simultaneously located in the most difficult sections of the channel
- The degree of complexity of the section (the presence of bends, turns, narrowing, etc.).

Table 2.5: Traffic safety factors for sections of canal.

Factor	Level of danger
1. Number of ships at the same time	
2–3	B
4–5	G
6–7	R
2. Overall ship danger rating	
Satisfactory	C
Acceptable	M
Very possibly unsatisfactory	Yel
3. Navigational complexity of the canal section	
Less difficult	C
Difficult	M
Very difficult	Yel

The navigation situation in this case, related to the movement of vessels between sections of the channel, is dynamically changing and requires decision making in the "on-line" mode. In this case, for the operational assessment of traffic safety, a table of traffic safety coefficients (Table 2.5) and a type of base coloroid (Figure 2.2) are proposed.

Another example of visualization is discussed in the paper [7] that deals with a medical application, The main idea behind this medical application is that we combine color information processing, and the use of mobile applications in decision-making processes, to increase the information content and efficiency of treatment and care for sick patients. For a family doctor caring for a group of patients, we offer a special mobile application that generates input data about the patient's condition in the form of information quanta of a certain color. The input data (12 in total) describes the general condition of the patient at the beginning of the day: temperature, pressure, general condition, condition of individual organs, and the like. Each color representation of each of the 12-input data assumes, for example, six ratings and a correspondingly specific color: very bad (high temperature, pressure, etc.) – red; threatening – yellow; alarming – magenta; more or less normal – green; good – cyan; very good – blue. The patient enters this color information into their mobile device, receives a summary score, and sends it to the doctor's mobile device. Thus, the doctor sees a generalized color assessment of the condition of his patients at the beginning of the working day.

2.2.2 Implementation examples for decision support systems

The use and dissemination of the results of this study is possible in various fields requiring the use of intelligent decision-making systems: military, medicine and production of medical devices; technical and infrastructural; sociological; environmental; emergency prevention, etc.

Let us consider the main structural and parametric features of the implementation of decision support systems using several examples related to marine infrastructure (considered in more detail in the works [12–20]), to aviation facilities [21–26], and to healthcare [7, 27, 28].

When operating marine infrastructure (ports, oil and gas terminals, shipping channels, etc.) with intensive traffic of transport and auxiliary vessels in limited water areas, problems arise with the safety of vessels and the environment – especially in non-standard scenarios, taking into account the human factor and the impact of intense random external disturbances on the vessel.

Improving flight safety requires: continuous improvement of automated procedures for pre-flight preparation of aircraft and crew; interactive human–machine control of aircraft in critical flight modes and situations; aircraft movement control at large airports with particularly intense traffic and extreme external conditions.

The DSS should include the creation of a database and its ranking by the degree of impact on aircraft safety and traffic at the airport, the output systems based on color optical logical networks, and visualization of the traffic control process with color information on dangerous traffic zones and aircraft states.

Improving patient health outcomes requires the continuous refinement of automated procedures for self-assessment, symptom tracking, and clinical decision support, for example, in cases of suspected or confirmed COVID-19. This process involves interactive, patient-focused interfaces for self-monitoring of key health indicators, coupled with remote healthcare oversight to identify critical symptoms early, and thus, to ensure timely medical interventions.

The decision support system should incorporate a structured database of clinically relevant parameters, prioritized based on their prognostic value for disease progression and for patient safety. The system will utilize color-coded optical logic networks to provide an intuitive visualization of the patient's health status, enabling both patients and healthcare professionals to rapidly assess potential health risks and take appropriate actions when necessary.

In [6], the authors proposed a structure of the DSS with the formation of an input database for a group of sea ports of Mykolaiv, based on the computational optical architecture proposed by the authors. The structure of the proposed DSS (Figure 2.5) includes two stages of control and decision-making. At the first stage, A, based on data on the entry of a vessel into the shipping channel, weather forecast, information on the total number of vessels in the channel, the DSS makes a decision on allowing entry or stopping the vessel until adverse transport and/or weather conditions change. At the second stage, B, the process of vessel movement in the shipping channel is assessed, taking into account information on each of the vessels in difficult sections of the channel, and decisions are made to improve the degree of traffic safety.

In the paper [10], a decision support system was developed with a significantly expanded database for large marine infrastructure facilities with significantly more intensive vessel traffic, including assessments of weather conditions and channel conditions, technical characteristics of the vessel, and the condition and qualifications of the crew, pilotage, and dispatch services.

A similar system in a more expanded form can be used to control the movement of airliners. The flight control dispatcher will see, in a certain color scheme, visual information about the movement of many aircraft in the airport's area of responsibility, with a corresponding safety assessment of the condition of each aircraft (based on an assessment of the technical condition of the aircraft itself and its crew, and perhaps, if necessary, passengers), as well as weather conditions and parameters of the section of the corresponding

Figure 2.5: Structure of the DSS.

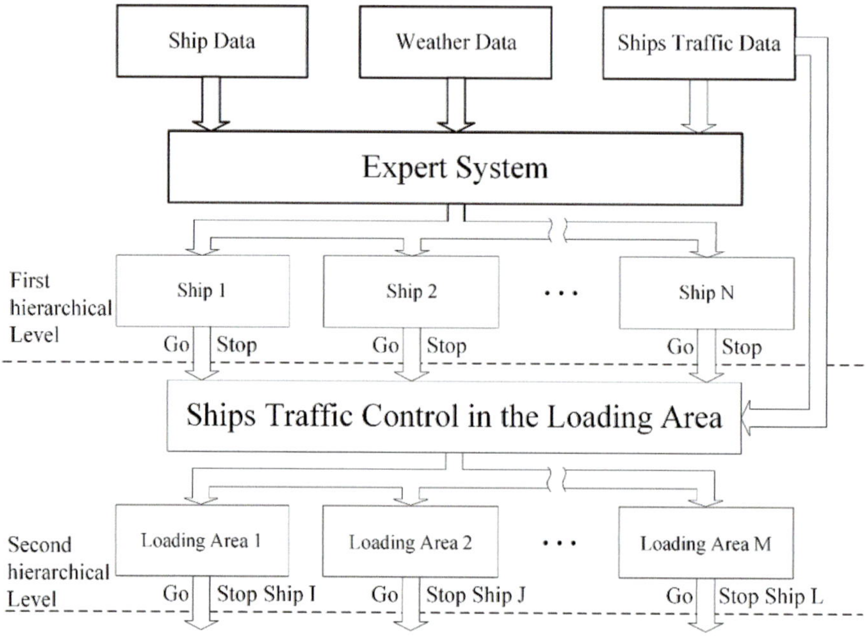

trajectory, taking into account its complexity and traffic intensity. Thus, the dispatcher has the opportunity to promptly respond to the degree of danger of the aircraft's movement, without being distracted in advance by a complex array of technical information.

Let us model, as a component of the DSS, the decision-making process for clearance for take-off using the example of the air crash that occurred in Denver (USA) on 15 November 1987 with the DC-9 aircraft, flight CO-1713. The investigation showed that the air accident occurred due to icing of the aircraft due to errors made by the air traffic controller and the crew. Let us form a database (Table 2.6) with the corresponding ranking of factors (estimated). The main ones will include estimates of weather conditions (wind), aircraft type and qualification of the airport controller; coordinating factors – the presence of snow cover, time of day, the level of traffic intensity at the airport, general condition of the aircraft and instruments, the number of aircraft in front of the runway, general condition of the pilots (possible fatigue from previous flights, emergency crew replacement, etc.); responsible factors –visibility on the airfield, pilot qualifications, staffing of the air traffic control service [26].

Table 2.6: Contributing factors to emergency aircraft take-off.

Factor	Level of danger	Factor	Level of danger
1. Cross wind speed		**4. Snow, cm**	
Light wind (1–3 m/s)	B	0–2	C
Moderate wind (4–6 m/s)	G	2–5	M
Strong wind (7–9 m/s)	R	>5	Yel
2. Aircraft type		**5. Time of day**	
Wide-body (4 engines)	B	Daylight	C
Wide or narrow-body (2 engines)	G	Dark time of day Night	M Yel
Light-engine	R	**6. Flight intensity**	
3. Dispatcher qualification (accident-free experience)		Low	C
High	B	Medium	M
Medium	G	High	Yel
Low	R		
7. General condition of the aircraft and its instruments		**10. Crew qualification (+2 pilots), h**	
Good	C	≥10,000	C
Satisfactory	M	5000–10,000	M
Acceptable	Yel	≤5,000	Yel
8. Number of aircraft in front of taxiway		**11. Visibility, m**	
1	C	>1600	C
2–3 >3	M Yel	700–1600 <700	M Yel

Table 2.6: Continued.

Factor	Level of danger	Factor	Level of danger
9. General condition of the pilots		**12. Staffing of the dispatch service**	
Good	C	Fully	C
Medium	Yel	Medium	M
Acceptable	M	Low	Yel

Based on the investigation scenario, it is possible to establish assessments of safety factors and the corresponding information fuzzy color quanta reflected in Table 2.6.

To obtain a decision on clearance for take-off of an aircraft, we will apply the basic logical coloroid (Figure 2.2) with color filter settings according to the investigation scenario and Table 2.6, the first section is **R** (cross wind), **G** (aircraft type), **B** (dispatcher qualification); the upper branch of the second section is **Yel** (Snow), **M** (time of day); the middle branch is **Yel** (flight intensity), **M** (general condition of the aircraft); the lower branch is **M** (number of aircraft in front of taxiway), **C** (general condition of the pilots); the third section is **C** (crew qualification), **M** (visibility), **Yel** (staffing of the dispatch service).

According to coloroid formulas, we write for the first section:

$$diag\,(R,\ 0,\ 0) + diag\,(0,\ G,\ 0) + diag\,(0,\ 0,\ B) = diag\,(R, G,\ B)$$

for the second section:

$$\begin{aligned}
&diag\,(R, G,\ B) \times diag\,(R,\ G,\ 0) \times diag\,(R,\ 0,\ B) = diag\,(R,\ 0,\ 0)\\
&diag\,(R, G,\ B) \times diag\,(R,\ G,\ 0) \times diag\,(R,\ 0,\ B) = diag\,(R,\ 0,\ 0)\\
&diag\,(R, G,\ B) \times diag\,(R,\ 0,\ B) \times diag\,(0,\ G,\ B) = diag\,(0,\ 0,\ B)\\
&diag\,(R,\ 0,\ 0) + diag\,(R,\ 0,\ 0) + diag\,(0,\ 0,\ B) = diag\,(R, 0,\ B)
\end{aligned}$$

and for the third section:

$$\begin{aligned}
&diag\,(R, 0,\ B) \times diag\,(0,\ G,\ B) \times diag\,(R,\ 0,\ B) \times diag\,(R, G,\ 0)\\
&\quad = diag\,(0,\ 0,\ 0)\,.
\end{aligned}$$

The result is the absence of a positive decision $\{Blc\}$, a ban on take-off.

It should be noted that in the case of a fully staffed control service (rating **M** or **C**), taking into account the high intensity of flights, the solution would be as follows:

$$diag\,(R, 0,\ B) \times diag\,(0,\ G,\ B) \times diag\,(R,\ 0,\ B) \times diag\,(R,\ 0,\ B)$$
$$= diag\,(0,\ 0, B)\,.$$

Result –$\{B\}$, take-off clearance.

It is therefore possible that air traffic control would have responded to the excessive delay of this aircraft after de-icing and would have alerted the crew to the need for additional de-icing action.

This example of the DSS component implementation is illustrative and covers the situational element of developing a scenario for automated aircraft movement control with a priority role for the human operator.

The COVID-19 self-assessment system is conceptualized to provide a comprehensive, color-coded representation of critical health indicators, facilitating both patient self-monitoring and healthcare professional oversight. This system adopts a methodologically rigorous approach to track symptoms, physiological metrics, and overall health status, thereby enabling a rapid and accurate appraisal of a patient's condition without the encumbrance of deciphering complex clinical data.

The self-assessment protocol encompasses 12 meticulously selected criteria. Each criterion is carefully chosen to reflect clinically significant symptoms and physiological markers. each stratified into six color-coded categories that denote varying levels of clinical concern. The chromatic scale ranges from blue (optimal health) to red (critical condition), thus enabling immediate perceptual recognition of health risks. This visual structure enhances patient capacity for early symptom recognition and informed decision-making regarding the necessity of medical intervention.

Integrated (Figure 2.6) into a broader decision support system (DSS), the self-assessment mechanism also assists healthcare providers by presenting synthesized, self-reported data that supports enhanced triage accuracy and facilitates remote patient monitoring. The selection of parameters is predicated upon an extensive review of contemporary empirical research, ensuring that the criteria are aligned with established COVID-19 pathophysiological patterns.

To show the system's utility, consider a simulated assessment derived from empirical analyses of hospitalized COVID-19 cohorts. Research consistently identifies indicators such as arterial hypoxemia, febrile responses, and persistent non-productive cough as reliable predictors of disease progression.

Figure 2.6: Structure of a medical DSS.

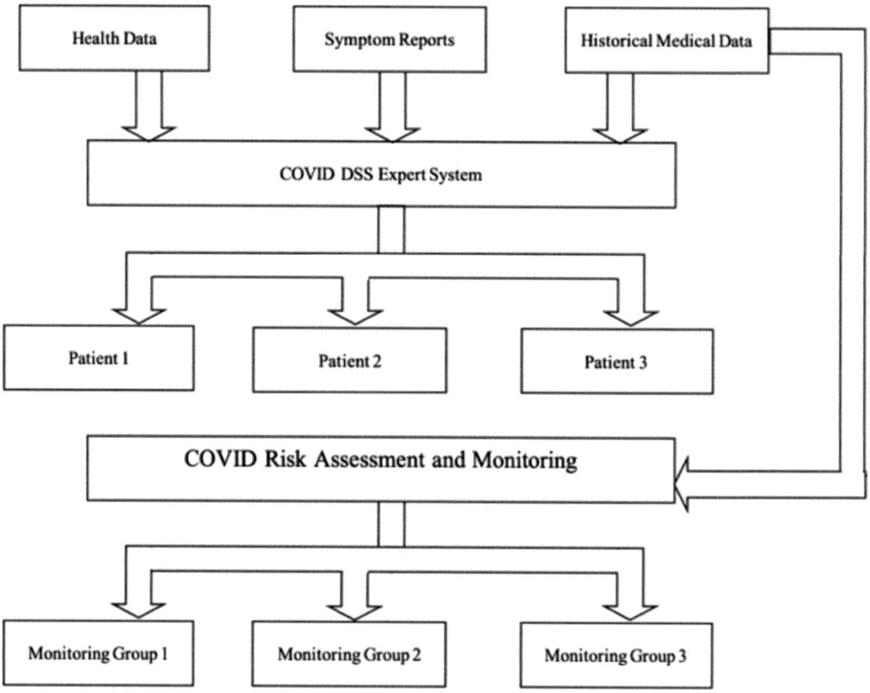

Consequently, the criteria set emphasizes variables like oxygen saturation, core body temperature, and respiratory distress patterns due to their high predictive value in clinical practice.

The Table 2.7 clearly outlines the prioritized criteria according to their clinical significance [27, 28], with color-coded categorizations that intuitively convey the severity of each symptom or physiological measure. For instance, an "oxygen saturation" level below 88% is classified in red, signifying a critical need for immediate medical attention, whereas measurements of 97% or above are represented in cyan or blue, indicative of optimal pulmonary function.

This self-assessment system fosters proactive patient engagement by equipping individuals with the tools to monitor their own health status, thus encouraging timely medical consultations in the presence of deterioration indicators. Simultaneously, it provides healthcare professionals with systematically organized, interpretable data to inform clinical decisions, particularly within telemedicine frameworks and remote healthcare infrastructures.

Table 2.7: Patient self-assessment criteria, color-coded.

Factor	Level of danger	Factor	Level of danger
1. Body temperature (°C)		**4. Heart rate (bpm)**	
36.0–36.6	B	60–75	C
36.7–37.1	G	76–95	M
≥38.1	R	>96	Yel
2. Oxygen saturation (SpO2, %)		**5. Blood pressure (mmHg)**	
99–98	B	110/75	C
97–94	G	120/85	M
97–94	R	≥140/90	Yel
3. Respiratory symptoms (self-reported)		**6. Breathing rate breaths/min)**	
No symptoms, no known exposure	B	12–18	C
Occasional cough, mild discomfort	G	19–24	M
Severe shortness of breath	R	>25	Yel
7. Sense of smell and taste		**10. Cough severity (self-reported)**	
Fully intact	C	No cough	C
Minor to noticeable distortion	M	Occasional to persistent dry cough	M
Severe reduction to complete loss	Yel	Severe cough with breathing issues	Yel
8. Energy level (self-reported)		**11. Chest pain or discomfort**	
Energetic, full of energy	C	No discomfort	C
Mild to significant fatigue	M	Occasional mild to sharp pain	M
Extreme exhaustion	Yel	Severe persistent pain	Yel

Table 2.7: Continued.

Factor	Level of danger	Factor	Level of danger
9. Headache frequency/severity		**12. Mental state (self-reported)**	
No headache	C	Calm, focused	C
Occasional to frequent moderate headaches	Yel	Mild anxiety to periodic confusion	M
Severe, debilitating headaches	M	Disorientation/confusion	Yel

Based on trusted medical sources [27], the following 12 criteria are essential for self-assessment in patients with confirmed or suspected COVID-19. Each criterion is categorized from very good to very bad, with corresponding color codes.

These criteria are aligned with guidelines from reputable health organizations and are crucial for monitoring and assessing the health status of individuals with COVID-19.

To determine the overall health risk level of a patient with suspected or confirmed COVID-19, we apply the structured self-assessment model with color-coded indicators. The initial assessment section includes **G** (oxygen saturation), **G** (body temperature), **G** (respiratory symptoms severity); the upper branch of the second section consists of **M** (heart rate), **C** (breathing rate); the middle branch includes **M** (energy level), **C** (cough severity); and the lower branch assesses **Yel** (headache frequency), **C** (chest pain/discomfort). The third section factors in **C** (mental state), **M** (sense of smell/taste), **M** (blood pressure levels).

Using the established formulas, we derive:

For the first section:

$$diag\,(0,\ \mathrm{G},\ 0) + diag\,(0,\ \mathrm{G},\ 0) + diag\,(0,\ \mathrm{G},\ 0) = diag\,(0,\ \mathrm{G},\ 0)\,.$$

This step evaluates the severity of respiratory symptoms in conjunction with oxygen saturation and body temperature.

For the second section:

$$diag\,(0,\ G,\ 0) \times diag\,(R,\ 0,\ B) \times diag\,(0,\ G, B) = diag\,(0,\ 0,\ 0)$$

$$diag\,(0,\ G,\ 0) \times diag\,(R,\ 0,\ B) \times diag\,(0,\ G, B) = diag\,(0,\ 0,\ 0)$$

$$diag\,(0,\ G,\ 0) \times diag\,(R,\ G,\ 0) \times diag\,(0,\ G,\ B) = diag\,(0,\ G,\ 0)$$

$$diag\,(0,\ 0,\ 0) + diag\,(0,\ 0,\ 0) + diag\,(0,\ G,\ 0) = diag\,(0,\ G,\ 0)\,.$$

This section analyses the interplay between heart rate, breathing rate, energy level, and cough severity.

For the third section:

$$diag\,(0,\ G,\ 0) \times diag\,(0,\ G,\ B) \times diag\,(R,\ 0,\ B) \times diag\,(R,\ 0,\ B) \\ = diag\,(0,\ 0,\ 0)\,.$$

The result indicates a $\{Blc\}$ status (absence of a decision) due to potentially ambiguous input information. It means that an input data needs to be collected anew and decision-making cycle – reattempted.

However, if sense of smell/taste is intact and blood pressure level is normal, the calculation becomes:

$$diag\,(0,\ G,\ 0) \times diag\,(0,\ G,\ B) \times diag\,(0,\ G,\ B) \times diag\,(0,\ G,\ B) \\ = diag\,(0,\ \mathrm{G}, 0)\,.$$

The outcome $\{G\}$ indicates a stable condition, where ongoing monitoring and symptomatic treatment are advisable without immediate hospitalization.

This implementation of the self-assessment system within a decision-support framework illustrates how structured logic can aid in clinical triage. It provides a rapid, systematic evaluation of patient status, ensuring timely intervention while minimizing unnecessary healthcare resource utilization.

2.3 Summary

The efficiency of the proposed optical architecture, the computational costs of the proposed approach and the most efficient modern digital processors were compared in this chapter. It was found that while FPGA hardware accelerates the DSS algorithm compared to conventional x86-64 and ARM processors, the coloroid device concept is even faster: it is approximately 10^7 times faster than an ARM processor, 10^5 times faster than an x86-64 one, and 30 times faster than FPGA. The advantage of the coloroid lies in its near-light-speed photonic principles, while the performance of the FPGA comes at the expense of high hardware costs and specialized software development expertise.

The above findings strengthen the idea that optical logic systems, based on hybrid fuzzy-color computing, expand the functional capabilities of decision support systems with vast input information. They're simple to implement, have high computing performance due to light speed, multi-parallel structure, and output visualization. They are switching gates practically for free, they resist noise, and they are efficient.

In this chapter, we presented an illustrative example of modelling fuzzy computations within the structure of components of decision-making. We also showed how easy it is to use an optical logical device in marine, aircraft and medical applications.

In addition to current use cases, developed color optical logic devices can be successfully used to improve the efficiency of intelligent automation systems for complex objects and processes in various other industries in order to increase the productivity and performance of high-quality technological complexes. These devices will improve the accuracy, speed, and reliability of the systems, expand their functionality and simplify the hardware and software implementation of fuzzy control and decision-making systems, in particular, systems that are used to automate industrial and mobile robots, unmanned aerial vehicles, floating vehicles and structures, thermal power plants, diagnostic processes and forecasting, etc.

References

[1] C. Cole, 'Optical and electrical programmable computing energy use comparison,' Optics Express, Vol. 29, Issue 9, pp. 13153-13170, 2021. DOI: 10.1364/OE.420027

[2] P. L. McMahon, 'The physics of optical computing,' Nat Rev Phys 5, pp. 717–734, 2023. https://doi.org/10.1038/s42254-023-00645-5

[3] M. Matuszewski, A. Prystupiuk, A. Opala, 'The role of all-optical neural networks,' arXiv:2306.06632v2, [cs.ET] 13 Jun 2023. https://doi.org/10.48550/arXiv.2306.06632

[4] J. L. Hennessy, D. A. Patterson, 'Computer Architecture: A Quantitative Approach,' 6th ed., Morgan Kaufmann Publishers, 2019.

[5] M. S. Chelva, S. V. Halse, 'A performance study of GPU, FPGA, DSP, and multicore processors for embedded vision systems,' ITSI Transactions on Electrical and Electronics Engineering, ITSI-TEEE, vol. 3, no. 5–6, pp. 61-66, 2015, http://irdindia.in/journal_itsi/pdf/vol3_iss5_6/13.pdf

[6] V. Timchenko, V. Kreinovich, Y. Kondratenko, V. Horbov, 'Effectiveness evaluations of optical color fuzzy computing,' in: Y. Kondratenko, A. Shevchenko (eds.) Research Tendencies and Prospect Domains for AI Development and Implementation, River Publishers, pp. 129–150, 2024. https://www.scopus.com/pages/publications/85202987186

[7] V. Timchenko, V. Kreinovich, Y. Kondratenko, 'Logical platforms for mobile application in decision support systems based on color information processing,' Journal of Mobile Multimedia, vol. 20, no. 3, pp. 679–698, 2024. https://doi.org/10.13052/jmm1550-4646.2037

[8] "Digital Signal Processing – DSP Slice – AMD Technical Information Portal," [Online]. Available: https://docs.amd.com/r/en-US/ug585-zynq-7000-SoC-TRM/Digital-Signal-Processing-DSP-Slice, [Accessed: Feb. 25, 2025].

[9] V. Timchenko, Yu. Kondratenko, V. Kreinovich, 'Decision support system for the safety of ship navigation based on optical color logic gates,' CEUR Workshop Proceedings, Vol. 3347, pp. 42-52, 2022. https://ceur-ws.org/Vol-3347/Paper_4.pdf

[10] V. Timchenko, V. Kreinovich, Y. Kondratenko, I. Demidov, 'Hierarchical decision support system for increasing maritime safety based on optical color computing architecture,' in: A. Shevchenko, Y. Kondratenko (eds.) Artificial Intelligence: Achievements and Recent Developments, River Publishers, pp. 197–229, 2025, in print.

[11] V. Timchenko, Y. Kondratenko, V. Kreinovich, 'The Architecture of Optical Logical Coloroid with Fuzzy Computing,' CEUR Workshop Proceedings, Vol. 3373, pp. 638-648, 2023, https://ceur-ws.org/Vol-3373/paper44.pdf

[12] V. L. Timchenko, Y. P. Kondratenko, 'Robust stabilization of marine mobile objects on the basis of systems with variable structure of feedbacks,' J. Autom. Inf. Sci., vol. 43, no. 6, pp. 16–29, 2011. DOI: 10.1615/JAutomatInfScien.v43.i6.20

[13] V. L. Timchenko, D. Lebedev, 'Algorithmic procedures synthesis of robust-optimal control for moving objects,' in: Y. P. Kondratenko, V. M. Kuntsevich, A. A. Chikrii, V. F. Gubarev, (eds.), Recent Developments in Automatic Control Systems, River Publishers, pp. 289–323, 2022. https://www.scopus.com/pages/publications/85149376557

[14] Y. Huang, L. Chen, P. Chen, R. Negenborn, P. Van Gelder, 'Ship collision avoidance methods: State-of-the-art,' Safety Science, vol. 121, pp. 451–473, 2020. https://doi.org/10.1016/j.ssci.2019.09.018

[15] T. Wang, Q. Wu, J. Zhang, B. Wu, Y. Wang, 'Autonomous decision-making scheme for multi-ship collision avoidance with iterative observation and inference,' Ocean Engineering, vol. 197, 106873, 2020. https://doi.org/10.1016/j.oceaneng.2019.106873

[16] K. Naus, 'Drafting route plan templates for ships on the basis of AIS historical data,' J. Navigation, vol. 73, no. 3, pp. 726–745, 2020. DOI:10.1017/S0373463319000948

[17] Y. P. Kondratenko, A. Roshanineshat, D. Simon, 'Safe navigation of an autonomous robot in dynamic and unknown environments,' in: Y. P. Kondratenko, V. M. Kuntsevich, A. A. Chikrii, V. F. Gubarev, (eds.),

Recent Developments in Automatic Control Systems, River Publishers, pp. 261–288, 2022. https://www.scopus.com/pages/publications/85149361738

[18] R. Fiskin, O. Atik, H. Kisi, E. Nasibov, T. A. Johansen, 'Fuzzy domain and meta-heuristic algorithm-based collision avoidance control for ships: Experimental validation in virtual and real environment,' Ocean Engineering, vol. 220, 108502, 2021. https://doi.org/10.1016/j.oceaneng.2020.108502

[19] Y. Kondratenko, S. Sidorenko, 'Ship Navigation in Narrowness Passes and Channels in Uncertain Conditions: Intelligent Decision Support,' in: P. Shi, J. Stefanovski, J., Kacprzyk (eds) Complex Systems: Spanning Control and Computational Cybernetics: Foundations, Studies in Systems, Decision and Control, vol. 414, pp. 475–493, 2022, Springer, Cham, https://doi.org/10.1007/978-3-030-99776-2_24

[20] T.A. Altameem, E.Y.M., Al Zu'bi, Y.P. Kondratenko, 'Computer Decision Making System for Increasing Efficiency of Ship's Bunkering Process,' Annals of DAAAM for 2010 & Proceeding of the 21th Int. DAAAM Symp. "Intelligent Manufacturing and Automation", (20-23 Oct., 2010, Zadar, Croatia), Published by DAAAM International, Vienna, Austria, pp. 0403-0404, 2010. https://www.daaam.info/Downloads/Pdfs/proceedings/proceedings_2010/20540_Annals_1_head.pdf

[21] S. Barber, 'Aviation situation awareness and decision information system,' US Patent 10,532,823 B1, 2020.

[22] T. Chatterjee, J. Cheng, B. Healy, M. Davies, 'A modeling framework for evaluating safety of complex aerospace systems,' AIAA Paper 2021-1802, 2021. [Online]. Available: https://doi.org/10.2514/6.2021-1802

[23] P. Gonçalves, J. Sobral, L. A. Ferreira, 'Unmanned aerial vehicle safety assessment modelling through Petri Nets,' Reliability Engineering and System Safety, vol. 167, pp. 383–393, 2017. www.elsevier.com/locate/ress

[24] I. Sidenko, A. Trukhov, G. Kondratenko, Y. Zhukov, Y. Kondratenko, 'Machine Learning for Unmanned Aerial Vehicle Routing on Rough Terrain,' in: Z. Hu, I. Dychka, M. He, M. (eds) Advances in Computer Science for Engineering and Education VI, ICCSEEA 2023, Lecture Notes on Data Engineering and Communications Technologies, Vol. 181, Springer, Cham, 2023, pp. 626–635. DOI:10.1007/978-3-031-36118-0_56

[25] A. Hobbs, 'Remotely Piloted Aircraft Systems, 'Human Factors in Aviation and Aerospace,' pp. 399–419, 2022. DOI:10.1016/B978-0-12-420139-2.00007-1

[26] 'Introduction to Aircraft Performance,' Flight Operations Support & Services, AIRBUS, 210 p., 2007.

[27] 'Online symptoms self-assessment during COVID-19 pandemic: an analysis of a COVID-19 portal responses from Canada,' National Library of

Medicine [Online]. https://pmc.ncbi.nlm.nih.gov/articles/PMC9156693/. [Accessed: Feb. 25, 2025].

[28] O. Kozlov, Y. Kondratenko, O. Skakodub, 'Comparative Analysis of Parametric Optimization Techniques: Fuzzy DSS for Medical Diagnostics,' in: S.N. Shahbazova, A.M. Abbasov, V. Kreinovich, J. Kacprzyk, I.Z. Batyrshin (eds) Recent Developments and the New Directions of Research, Foundations, and Applications. Studies in Fuzziness and Soft Computing, vol. 423, pp. 193-201, 2023, Springer, Cham, https://doi.org/10.1007/978-3-031-23476-7_17

Index

For Product Safety Concerns and Information please contact our
EU representative GPSR@taylorandfrancis.com Taylor & Francis
Verlag GmbH, Kaufingerstraße 24, 80331 München, Germany